GCSE 9–1
BIOLOGY
EXAM PRACTICE
FOR ALL EXAM BOARDS

Kayan Parker

Author Kayan Parker
Editorial team Haremi Ltd
Series designers emc design ltd
Typesetting York Publishing Solutions Pvt. Ltd., and Newgen KnowledgeWorks (P) Ltd, Chennai, India
Illustrations York Publishing Solutions Pvt. Ltd., and Newgen KnowledgeWorks (P) Ltd, Chennai, India
App development Hannah Barnett, Phil Crothers and Haremi Ltd

Designed using Adobe InDesign
Published by Scholastic Education, an imprint of Scholastic Ltd, Book End, Range Road, Witney,
Oxfordshire, OX29 0YD
Registered office: Westfield Road, Southam, Warwickshire CV47 0RA
www.scholastic.co.uk

Printed by Bell & Bain Ltd, Glasgow
© 2017 Scholastic Ltd
1 2 3 4 5 6 7 8 9 7 8 9 0 1 2 3 4 5 6

British Library Cataloguing-in-Publication Data
A catalogue record for this book is available from the British Library.
ISBN 978-1407-17687-1

Acknowledgements

The publishers gratefully acknowledge permission to reproduce the following copyright material:

Photos: p8 Heiti Paves/Shutterstock; p11 Dlumen/Shutterstock; p13 and 15 Jose Luis Calvo/Shutterstock;
p82 grass-lifeisgood/Shutterstock; p15: Source: Health chart, developed by the National Center for Health Statistics in
collaboration with the National Center for Chronic Disease Prevention and Health Promotion (2000) from the Centre for Disease
Control National Center for Health Statistics; p29: Source: Australian Institute of Health and Welfare, reproduced under a
Creative Commons (CC) BY 3.0 licence; p30: Contains public sector information licensed under the Open Government Licence
v3.0; p33: Source: 'Comprehensive care with antiretroviral therapy for injecting-drug users associates to low community viral
load and restriction of HIV outbreak' © 2012 Kivelä, P et al; licensee International AIDS Society, Creative Commons (CC) BY 3.0
licence; p38: Source: https://sites.google.com/site/livingithealthy/jointpain; p59: Source: https://sofi avenanzetti. wordpress.
com/2014/03/23/stiffness-and-hormones/; p81, top: adapted from worksheet 'Toxic chemicals and food chains 2', http://www.
sciwebhop.net, © Pearson Education Limited 2002; p81, bottom: adapted from Odum, Fundamentals of Ecology, Saunders,
1953; p100: Source: Quandl. IMF data published by the ODA under an open data licence; p105: Reaction graph, reproduced
under a Creative Commons (CC) BY 3.0 licence.

Every effort has been made to trace copyright holders for the works reproduced in this book, and the publishers apologise for
any inadvertent omissions.

Note from the publisher:

Please use this product in conjunction with the official specification that you are following and sample assessment materials for
the exam board that will be setting your examinations. Ask your teacher if you are unsure where to find them. Mapping grids
showing you which content you need to know for the main specifications are found online at www.scholastic.co.uk/gcse.

The marks and star ratings have been suggested by our subject experts, but they are to be used as a guide only.

Answer space has been provided, but you may need to use additional paper for your workings.

Contents

CELL BIOLOGY

Topic 1

Eukaryotes and prokaryotes	8
Animal and plant cells	9
Cell specialisation and differentiation	10
Microscopy	11
Culturing microorganisms	12
Using a light microscope	13
Investigating the effect of antiseptics or antibiotics	14
Mitosis and the cell cycle	15
Stem cells	16
Diffusion	17
Osmosis	18
Investigating the effect of a range of concentrations of salt or sugar solutions on the mass of plant tissue	19
Active transport	20

TISSUES, ORGANS AND ORGAN SYSTEMS

Topic 2

The human digestive system and enzymes	21
Food tests	23
The effect of pH on amylase	24
The heart	25
The lungs	26
Blood vessels and blood	27
Coronary heart disease	28
Health issues and effect of lifestyle	29
Cancer	30
Plant tissues	31
Transpiration and translocation	32

INFECTION AND RESPONSE

Topic 3

Communicable (infectious) diseases	33
Viral and bacterial diseases	34
Fungal and protist diseases	35
Human defence systems	36
Vaccination	37
Antibiotics and painkillers	38
New drugs	39
Monoclonal antibodies and their uses	40
Plant diseases and defences	41

BIOENERGETICS

Topic 4

Photosynthesis	42
Rate of photosynthesis	43
Investigating the effect of light intensity on the rate of photosynthesis	44
Uses of glucose	45
Respiration and metabolism	46
Response to exercise	47

HOMEOSTASIS AND RESPONSE

Topic 5

Homeostasis	48
The human nervous system and reflexes	49
Investigating the effect of a factor on human reaction time	50
The brain and the eye	51
Focusing the eye	52
Control of body temperature	53
Human endocrine system	54
Control of blood glucose concentration	55

Contents

Diabetes 56
Maintaining water and nitrogen balance in the body 57
Dialysis 58
Hormones in human reproduction 59
Contraception 60
Using hormones to treat infertility 61
Negative feedback 62
Plant hormones 63
Investigating the effect of light or gravity on the growth of
    newly germinated seedlings 64

Topic 6

INHERITANCE, VARIATION AND EVOLUTION

Sexual and asexual reproduction 65
Meiosis 66
DNA and the genome 67
DNA structure 68
Protein synthesis 69
Genetic inheritance 70
Inherited disorders 71
Variation 72
Evolution 73
Selective breeding 74
Genetic engineering and cloning 75
Evolution and speciation 76
The understanding of genetics 77
Classification 78

Topic 7

ECOLOGY

Communities 79
Abiotic and biotic factors 80
Adaptations 82
Food chains 83
Measuring species 84
Investigating the relationship between organisms
    and their environment 85
The carbon cycle, nitrogen cycle and water cycle 86
Decomposition 87
Investigating the effect of temperature on the rate of decay 88
Impact of environmental change 89
Biodiversity 90
Global warming 91
Maintaining biodiversity 92
Trophic levels and pyramids of biomass 93
Food production and biotechnology 94

PAPER 1 95

ANSWERS 104

How to use this book

This Exam Practice Book has been produced to help you revise for your 9–1 GCSE in biology. Written by an expert and packed full of exam-style questions for each subtopic, along with full practice papers, it will get you exam ready!

The best way to retain information is to take an active approach to revision. Don't just read the information you need to remember – do something with it! Transforming information from one form into another and applying your knowledge will ensure that it really sinks in. Throughout this book you'll find lots of features that will make your revision practice an active, successful process.

EXAM-STYLE QUESTIONS

Exam-style questions for each subtopic ramped in difficulty.

For mapping grids to show you exactly what you need to know for your specification and tier, go to www.scholastic. co.uk/gcse

DO IT!

Tasks that support your understanding and analysis of a question.

WORKIT!

Worked examples with model solutions to help you see how to answer a tricky question.

Callouts Step-by-step guidance to build understanding.

NAILIT!

Tips to help you perform in the exam.

STRETCHIT!

Questions or concepts that stretch you further and challenge you with the most difficult content.

★ STAR RATING ★

A quick visual guide to indicate the difficulty of the question, with 1 star representing the least demanding and 5 stars signposting the most challenging questions.

MARKS (5 marks)

Each question has the number of marks available to help you target your response.

PRACTICE PAPERS

Full mock-exam papers to enable you to have a go at a complete paper before you sit the real thing!

For an additional practice paper, visit: www.scholastic.co.uk/gcse

Use the Biology Revision Guide for All Boards alongside the Exam Practice Book for a complete revision and practice solution. Written by a subject expert to match the new specifications, the Revision Guide uses an active approach to revise all the content you need to know!

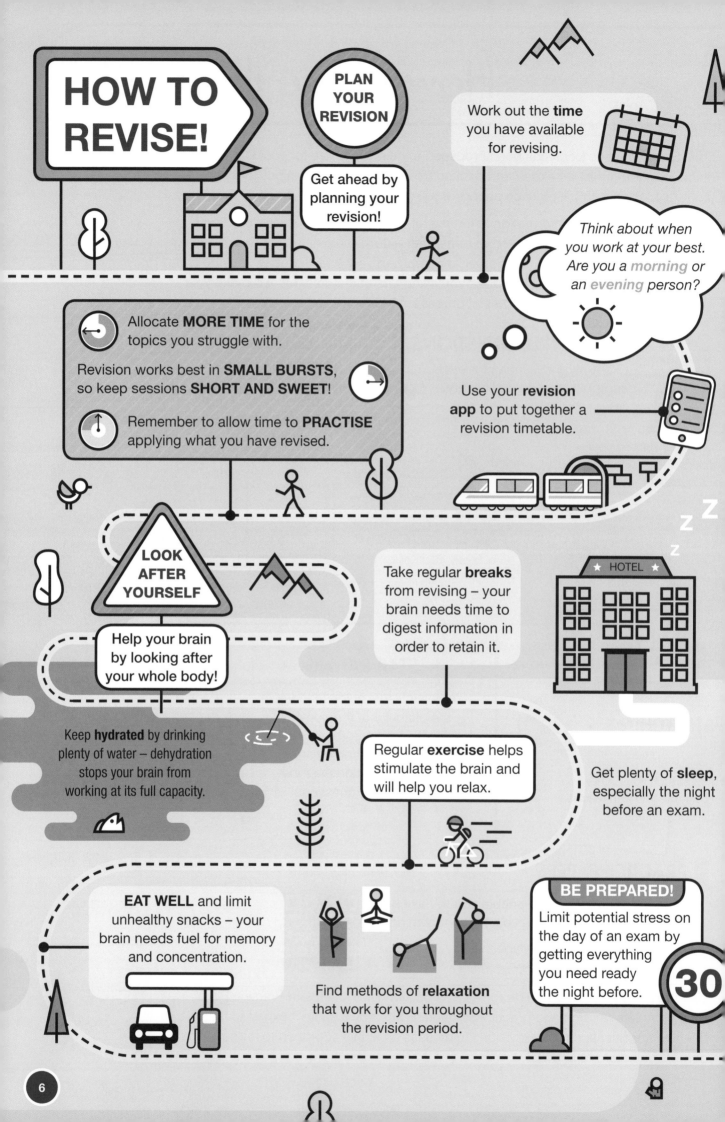

HOW TO REVISE!

PLAN YOUR REVISION

Get ahead by planning your revision!

Work out the **time** you have available for revising.

Think about when you work at your best. Are you a morning or an evening person?

Allocate **MORE TIME** for the topics you struggle with.

Revision works best in **SMALL BURSTS**, so keep sessions **SHORT AND SWEET!**

Remember to allow time to **PRACTISE** applying what you have revised.

Use your **revision app** to put together a revision timetable.

LOOK AFTER YOURSELF

Help your brain by looking after your whole body!

Take regular **breaks** from revising – your brain needs time to digest information in order to retain it.

HOTEL

Keep **hydrated** by drinking plenty of water – dehydration stops your brain from working at its full capacity.

Regular **exercise** helps stimulate the brain and will help you relax.

Get plenty of **sleep**, especially the night before an exam.

EAT WELL and limit unhealthy snacks – your brain needs fuel for memory and concentration.

Find methods of **relaxation** that work for you throughout the revision period.

BE PREPARED!

Limit potential stress on the day of an exam by getting everything you need ready the night before.

30

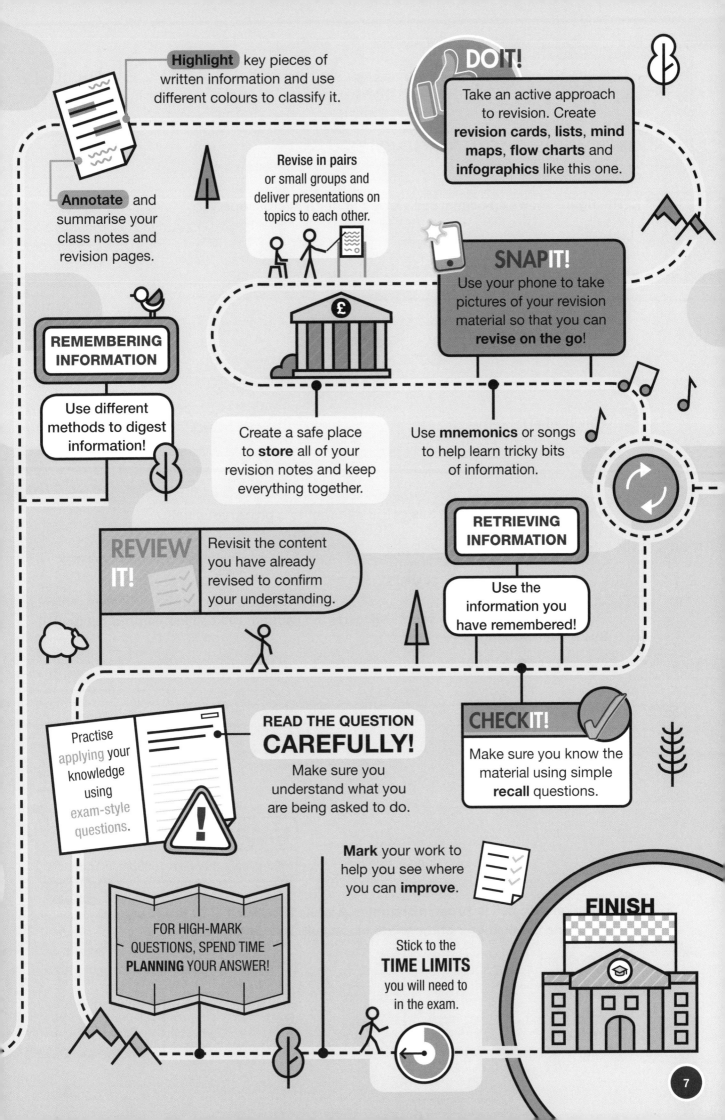

Eukaryotes and prokaryotes

(1) **The figure shows an animal cell viewed under a microscope.**

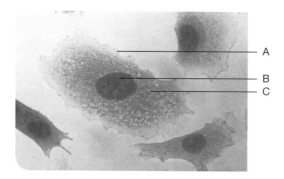

— A
— B
— C

a **Which label is:**

- the nucleus? ......B......

- the cytoplasm? ......C...... (2 marks, ★)

b **Name two ways in which this cell is different to a prokaryotic cell.** (2 marks, ★★)

i ......IT HAS A NUCLEUS......

ii ......IT HAS NO PLASMIDS......

c **The central cell is 0.1 mm wide. Calculate the width of the cell in micrometres (μm). Show your working.** (2 marks, ★★★)

0.1 ×1000 = 100

......100...... μm

NAILIT!

Remember there are 1000 μm in 1 mm.

d **A prokaryotic cell is 10 μm in diameter. A white blood cell is 60 times bigger. Calculate the diameter of the white blood cell. Tick one box.** (1 mark, ★★★)

60 000 nm	
6000 μm	
60 mm	
0.6 mm	✓

10 × 60 = 600 μM

600 ⁄ 1000 = 0.6 mm

Animal and plant cells

(1) Match each function to the correct sub-cellular structure. One has been done for you.

(3 marks, ★)

Cytoplasm

Absorbs sunlight for photosynthesis — Nucleus

Contains the genetic material of the cell — Permanent vacuole

Provides strength to the cell — Cell membrane

Filled with cell sap to keep the plant turgid — Chloroplasts

Cellulose cell wall

DO IT!

Mark the student's answer below using the mark scheme, and suggest how to improve the answer.

What are the differences between animal and plant cells? (3 marks, ★★)

Plant cells have a cell wall, chloroplasts and

vacuoles, and animal cells do not.

MARK SCHEME
Plant cells have a cellulose cell wall (1),
chloroplasts (1) and a permanent vacuole (1), and
animal cells do not.

Number of marks for student's answer:

2

How to improve the answer:

ONE PERMANENT VACUOLE, NOT

VACUOLES.

(2) The image shows a plant cell.

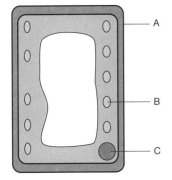

a **Label the structures A, B and C.** (3 marks, ★★)

A   CELL WALL

B   CHLOROPLAST

C   NUCLEUS

b **Explain why cells near the surface of a leaf contain more of structure B.** (2 marks, ★★)

CHLOROPLASTS TAKE SUNLIGHT AND TURN IT TO FOOD

(GLUCOSE) AND THE SURFACES OF A LEAF GETS MORE

SUNLIGHT

NAILIT!

If a question is worth two marks, then you must make two separate points.

Cell specialisation and differentiation

1. a **Which of these is a feature of sperm cells? Tick one box.**
   (1 mark, ★)

Long axon	
Many mitochondria	✓
Large surface area	
Hollow tube	

   b **Name two types of cell that work as a tissue.** (2 marks, ★★)

   i ....

   ii ....

   c **Ciliated epithelial cells have cilia on their top surface. Explain why this is important for their function.**
   (2 marks, ★★★)

   MORE SURFACE AREA

   ....

DO IT!

Mark the student's answer below using the mark scheme, and suggest how to improve the answer.

What is the definition of a tissue? (2 marks, ★★)

A group of cells working together to perform

a particular function.

MARK SCHEME
A group of similar cells working together (1) to perform a particular function. (1)

Number of marks for student's answer:

1

How to improve the answer:

SIMILAR CELLS, NOT JUST CELLS.

....

2. a **What is a stem cell?** (1 mark, ★)

   AN UNSPECIALIZED CELL

NAILIT!

Remember that phloem cells transport sugars around the plant.

   b **Where would you expect to find a large number of stem cells? Tick one box.** (1 mark, ★)

Embryo	✓
Mature animal	
Mature plant	

NAILIT!

This question asks you to apply your knowledge and understanding of cell differentiation and stem cells to a situation that you may not have studied before. Remember to use scientific terminology.

   c **Using your knowledge of cell differentiation, suggest how stem cells could be used to make new organs for transplant.** (4 marks, ★★★)

   AS STEM STEM CELLS ARE

   UNDIFFERENTIATED, THEY CAN BECOME ANY CELL VIA COPYING.

   WE CAN THEREFORE TAKE STEM CELLS, AND MAKE A CLONE

   OF THE NEW ORGAN.

Microscopy

(1) **This image shows some cells seen through an electron microscope.**

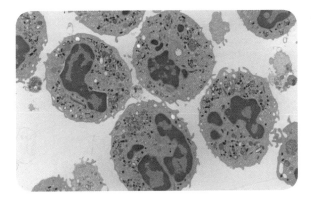

a **A student thinks the cells are plant cells. Use features in the image to explain whether the student is right.** (2 marks, ★★)

THE IMAGE SHOWS CELLS WITH

WHAT LOOK LIKE A PERMANENT

VACUOLES, SO THEY ARE CORRECT.

b **In another image, a cell is 0.5 μm wide but appears to be 5 cm wide. Calculate the magnification of the electron microscope.** (3 marks, ★★★)

$0.5 \times \div 1000 = 0.0005 \text{ mm}$

$\div 10 = 0.00005 \text{ cm}$

$5/0.00005 = 100\,000$

NAILIT!

Electron microscopes have a high magnification. Your answer should be in the range of × 50 000 – 500 000. Remember to convert the size of the image into micrometres (μm). 1 cm = 10 mm and 1 mm = 1000 μm

Magnification = $\underline{\times 100\,000}$

(2) **What are the advantages of using an electron microscope rather than a light microscope?** (2 marks, ★★★)

AN ELECTRON MICROSCOPE HAS SIGNIFICANTLY MORE RESOLUTION

AND MAGNIFICATION THAN A LIGHT MICROSCOPE, WHICH ALLOWS

IT TO SEE IN GREATER DETAIL

(3) **One early microscope had a magnification of × 200. How large would a 10 μm cell have appeared to be? Show your working.** (3 marks, ★★)

$m = \dfrac{i}{r}$

$i = m \times r$

$200 \times 10 = 2000$

Size of image = $\underline{2000}$

Culturing microorganisms

(1) **a Name the process by which bacteria divide.** (1 mark, ★)

MITOSIS

b Plan a method to produce an uncontaminated culture of bacteria on an agar plate.
(4 marks, ★★★)

STERILIZE A SPREADER AND EVENLY SPREAD THE BACTERIAL

SOLUTION ONTO THE AGAR. SEAL THE PLATE WITH THE LID

AND TAPE, AND INCUBATE AT THE APPROPRIATE TEMPERATURE.

> **NAILIT!**
>
> Remember to include aseptic techniques.

c One colony of bacteria has a diameter of 5mm. What is the cross-sectional area of the colony? Use the formula πr^2. (3 marks, ★★★)

$\pi = 3.142$

r = the radius of the colony $\pi \times 2.5^2 =$

Cross-sectional area = 19.6375

d There were ten bacteria in the original colony. The bacteria divided once every 30 minutes. How many bacteria were in the colony after 12 hours? (3 marks, ★★)

2 × 12 = 24

10 × 2²⁴ =

Number of bacteria = 167772160

> **NAILIT!**
>
> Don't forget to write very large numbers in **standard form**.

Using a light microscope

1 **The image shows some blood cells as seen through a light microscope.**

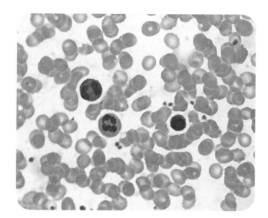

a **Describe how to focus the microscope so that the nuclei of the cells are clearly visible.** (3 marks, ★★)

FOCUS ON THE LOWEST RESOLUTION ~~KNOW~~ WITH THE COARSE FOCUS. CHANGE TO A HIGHER RES AND ADJUST.

b **Explain why microscope slides are often stained.** (2 marks, ★★)

USING A STAIN ~~BRA~~ MAKES IT EASIER TO SEE DETAIL DUE TO COLOUR

c **The eyepiece lens of the light microscope has a magnification of × 10. The objective lens has a magnification of × 40. What is the magnification of the microscope?** (1 mark, ★★)

Magnification = × 400

2 **An investigation looked at the effect of mitotic inhibitors on cell division. Cells were grown for 12 hours in one of two conditions: with or without mitotic inhibitor. The cells were then counted. The table shows the results.**

	Number of cells after 12 hours			
	1	2	3	Mean
With mitotic inhibitor	12	10	11	11
Without mitotic inhibitor	108	110	106	108

MATHS SKILLS

To work out the mean, add the three numbers in the row together and divide by three.

a **Complete the missing data in the table.** (2 marks, ★★)

b **Name two variables that must be kept constant during the investigation.** (2 marks, ★★★)

i TYPE OF CELL

ii TIME GROWN

c **Suggest one improvement to the investigation.** (1 mark, ★)

REPEAT MORE

Investigating the effect of antiseptics or antibiotics

(1) The image shows the results of an investigation into different types of antiseptics. Bacteria were grown on a sterile agar plate. Five antiseptics (A–E) were then added to the agar plate.

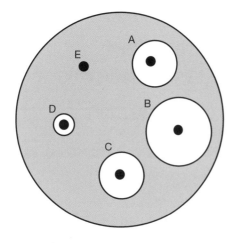

a Which antiseptic was most effective at inhibiting bacterial growth? (1 mark, ★★)

B

b Why was a **sterile** agar plate used? (1 mark, ★)

TO AVOID CONTAMINATION MESSING

WITH THE RESULTS

c Antiseptic D has a small clear area around it, 8 mm in diameter. Explain what this shows. (2 marks, ★★)

THE ANTISEPTIC KILLED FEW BACTERIA ,AND WAS NOT VERY

EFFECTIVE.

NAILIT!

Think about why aseptic techniques are important when culturing microorganisms.

NAILIT!

Use **zones of inhibition** in your answer.

d Calculate the cross-sectional area (*A*) of the clear area around antiseptic D, using the formula *A* = π*r*². (3 marks, ★★★)

$\pi 4^2 = 50.272$

MATHS SKILLS

π = 3.142

The radius is half the diameter.

Cross-sectional area = 50.272 mm²

Mitosis and the cell cycle

1 **a** **Match each stage of the cell cycle with what happens in that stage.** (3 marks, ★★)

G2 phase   The cell divides into two daughter cells.

S phase   Chromosomes are replicated.

                            Physical process of cell division.

M phase   Sub-cellular structures are replicated.

Cytokinesis   Chromosomes are checked.

b **Why do the sub-cellular structures need to double?** (2 marks, ★★)

TO   PROVIDE   NEW   CELLS   TO

REPLACE   ~~DM~~ ~~DM~~ DAMAGED   ONES

OR   OLD   ONES

NAILIT!

Think about what will happen to the cell at the end of mitosis.

2 **This image shows onion cells going through mitosis, as seen with a light microscope.**

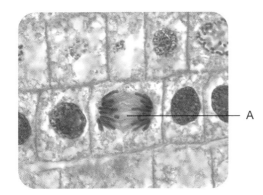

a i **Draw and label the cell marked A.** (2 marks, ★★★)

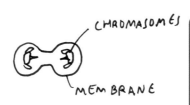

CHROMASOMES

MEMBRANE

A

NAILIT!

Draw the cell with a pencil. Label as many features as you can see.

ii **Describe what is happening inside the cell.** (2 marks, ★★★)

THE   ~~CHROMASOM~~ CHRUMAYOMES   ARE

PULLING   ODPOSITELY ~~TO~~ + SPLITTING

3 **This graph shows the percentile growth curve for baby girls aged 0–36 months.**

What is the mass in pounds of a baby girl on the 75th percentile line at 18 months? (1 mark, ★★★)

2 6 lb

Weight-for-age percentiles: Girls, birth to 36 months
CDC Growth Charts: United States

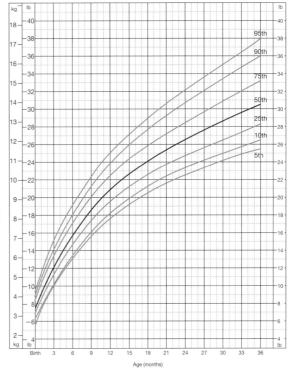

Stem cells

(1) **Which of the following statements about stem cells is/are true? Tick one box.** (1 mark, ★)

1 **Stem cells are undifferentiated cells.**

2 **Stem cells can become any type of cell.**

3 **Stem cells can only divide a certain number of times.**

A Statement 1 only	
B Statements 1 and 2 only	✓
C Statements 2 and 3 only	
D All of the statements	

(2) **Name two uses of stem cells.** (2 marks, ★★)

i   CLONING ORGANS FOR TRANSPLANT

ii   MEDICAL RESEARCH

(3) **Some areas of plants contain tissue that has the same properties as stem cells. Name this tissue and state where it is found in the plant.** (2 marks, ★★)

(4) **Describe two advantages and two disadvantages of using stem cells in medicine.** (4 marks, ★★★)

NAILIT!

Advantages and disadvantages can be practical, social and/or ethical.

WORKIT!

What are the advantages in using embryonic stems cells (as opposed to adult stem cells) in the growth of tissue/therapeutic cloning? (2 marks, ★★★)

Embryonic stem cells can develop into any type of cell in the body. (1)

Embryonic stem cells can be used to grow organs that will not be rejected by a patient's body/immune system. (1)

Diffusion

(1) a **What is diffusion?** (2 marks, ★★)

....

....

b **Give an example of diffusion in the human body.** (1 mark, ★)

....

NAILIT!

Think about an exchange surface in the body.

(2) a **Organism A has a surface area of 24 cm² and a volume of 8 cm³. Organism B has a surface area of 96 cm² and a volume of 64 cm³. Which has the smallest surface area to volume ratio?** (3 marks, ★★★)

....

....

....

MATHS SKILLS

Simplify the surface area to volume ratio to the lowest figure, e.g. 12:2 can be written as 6:1.

The organism with the smallest difference between the surface area and the volume has the smaller surface area to volume ratio.

b **Why do organisms with a small surface area to volume ratio need specialised exchange surfaces?** (3 marks, ★★)

....

....

....

(3) **A piece of Visking tubing is being used as a model cell. Plan an experiment to show that glucose solution inside the model cell diffuses into the surrounding pure water. Explain what factors you would need to know to calculate the rate of diffusion (refer to Fick's law).** (5 marks, ★★★★)

....

....

....

....

....

Osmosis

(1) **Define osmosis.** (2 marks, ★★)

....

....

(2) **An animal cell is placed in a concentrated solution. In which direction will water move?**
(1 mark, ★)

....

(3) **A disc of plant tissue has a mass of 10 g. It is placed in a dilute solution for 6 hours. The mass is measured again and found to be 14 g. What is the percentage increase in mass? Show your working.** (3 marks, ★★★)

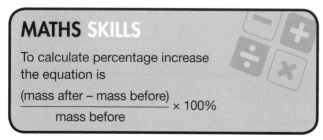

MATHS SKILLS

To calculate percentage increase the equation is

$$\frac{(\text{mass after} - \text{mass before})}{\text{mass before}} \times 100\%$$

Percentage increase in mass = ... %

(4) **The graph below shows the percentage change in mass of potato cubes placed in sugar solutions of different concentrations.**

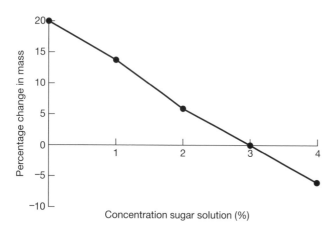

Percentage change in mass

Concentration sugar solution (%)

a **Using the graph, identify the sugar concentration at which the sugar concentration inside the potato cells is the same as in the sugar solution. Justify your answer.** (2 marks, ★★★)

....

....

....

....

....

....

b **At the concentration you gave in (a), why is the sugar concentration inside the potato cells the same as in the sugar solution?** (1 mark, ★★)

....

....

Investigating the effect of a range of concentrations of salt or sugar solutions on the mass of plant tissue

(1) The table below shows data collected after slices of cucumber were placed in salt solutions of different concentration for 12 hours.

a Complete the table to show the percentage change in mass to **one decimal place**.
(4 marks, ★★)

> Carefully check the column headings and numbers in the table. Is anything missing? Has all the data been recorded to the same number of decimal places?

Salt solution concentration (%)	Mass of cucumber slice at start (g)	Mass of cucumber slice after 12 hours	Percentage change in mass (%)
0	4.0	5.4	35.0
1	4.2	4.9	
2	4.1	4.1	
4	4	3.0	
5	4.1	2.7	

b **Correct any mistakes in the table.** (2 marks, ★★★)

Mistake 1: _____   Correction 1: _____

Mistake 2: _____   Correction 1: _____

c **On a separate piece of graph paper, draw a graph showing the percentage change in mass at different salt concentrations.** (4 marks, ★★★)

d **Using the graph, what is the percentage change in mass of the cucumber slice at 3% salt concentration?** (1 mark, ★★)

....

....

....

> **NAILIT!**
>
> Depending on your exam board you may need to refer to water potential in your answer. Make sure you check your mapping grid.

e **The cucumber slice at 5% salt solution was examined under a light microscope. Describe how you would expect the cells to look and explain why.**
(3 marks, ★★)

....

....

....

....

Active transport

(1) **What is active transport?** (2 marks, ★★)

....

....

(2) **Give one example of active transport in plants.** (1 mark, ★)

....

(3) **Complete the table to show the features of diffusion, osmosis and active transport. For each type of movement, tick the statement(s) that are true. The first row has been done for you.** (3 marks, ★★)

Type of movement	Involves the movement of water	Involves the movement of particles	The movement is from dilute solution to concentrated solution	The movement is from concentrated solution to dilute solution
Diffusion		✓		✓
Osmosis				
Active transport				

(4) **Suggest why cells in the wall of the small intestine contain many mitochondria.** (3 marks, ★★★)

....

....

NAILIT!

Remember that respiration is carried out in mitochondria.

(5) **Carrot seedlings were grown in aerobic and anaerobic conditions. The amount of potassium ions absorbed by the seedlings was measured every 30 minutes. The results are shown in the table below.**

Time (minutes)	Total amount of potassium ions absorbed (arbitrary units)	
	With oxygen (aerobic)	Without oxygen (anaerobic)
0	0	0
30	210	120
60	280	170
90	340	185
120	380	210
150	420	230

a **Compare the amount of potassium ions taken up by seedlings grown in each condition.** (1 mark, ★★)

....

b **Explain the pattern of potassium uptake in each condition.** (3 marks, ★★★)

....

....

c **How could this investigation be made more valid and reliable?** (2 marks, ★★)

....

....

Tissues, organs and organ systems

The human digestive system and enzymes

(1) a **Name two organs in the human digestive system.** (2 marks, ★)

i .... ii ....

b **Describe what happens to food as it moves through the human digestive system.** (5 marks, ★★★)

....

....

....

....

....

....

> **NAILIT!**
>
> Include any substances that are added to the food as it passes through the digestive system.

(2) a **The table below shows types of enzyme used in digestion. Fill in the missing information.** (3 marks, ★★)

Enzymes	Substrate	Products
	carbohydrates	sugars
proteases		amino acids
lipases	lipids	

b **Explain the role of bile in digestion.** (2 marks, ★★★★)

....

....

....

> **WORKIT!**
>
> Where in the body are proteases made? (1 mark, ★)
>
> Proteases are made in the stomach/pancreas. (1)

(3) **Describe how the amount of energy in food can be measured.** (2 marks, ★★)

....

....

(4) a **What does the term biological catalyst mean?** (1 mark, ★★)

....

b **The enzyme amylase breaks down starch. Explain why amylase would not break down lipids.** (2 marks, ★★★★)

....

....

c **Amylase has an optimum pH of 7. Describe and explain what would happen to amylase at a pH of 2.** (3 marks, ★★★★)

....

....

....

(5) **Catalase is an enzyme that breaks down hydrogen peroxide into water and oxygen. If hydrogen peroxide is converted into 24 cm³ of oxygen in three minutes, what is the rate of reaction? Show your working.** (2 marks, ★★★)

....

....

MATHS SKILLS

To calculate the rate of reaction per minute, divide the volume of oxygen produced by the time (number of minutes).

NAILIT!

Topic link: Enzymes are proteins so you may also be asked about protein synthesis in exam questions about digestion or enzymes.

(6) **Sketch the shape of the rate-of-reaction graph you would expect to see for a reaction with a fixed concentration of enzymes, but limitless substrate. Explain the shape of your graph.** (3 marks, ★★★★)

....

....

....

....

....

....

Food tests

(1) **Match each food type to its test.**
(3 marks, ★★)

Starch		Biuret test
Protein		Benedict's test
		Iodine test
Lipid		Emulsion test

(2) **A food sample turns lilac after testing. Identify which test was used, and explain what the result shows.** (2 marks, ★★★★)

Name of test:

....

What the result shows:

....

....

....

(3) **A student wants to test a sample for the presence of glucose. Describe the procedure that the student should use.** (4 marks, ★★★)

....

....

....

....

NAILIT!

Describe the steps that the student should follow to carry out the test, and what the results would show.

(4) **Two students use iodine solution to test a solution at two different times. After one minute, the solution turns blue-black. After five minutes, the solution has turned orange.**

Student A says that the solution must have contained starch and amylase, and the amylase must have digested the starch into maltose.

Student B says that the iodine solution might not be working properly and that one of the results must not be correct.

Explain how you could work out who is correct. (4 marks, ★★★★★)

....

....

....

....

....

The effect of pH on amylase

(1) **Describe the role of amylase in humans.** (2 marks, ★★★)

....

....

(2) **Some students investigated the effect of pH on amylase. The graph shows their results.**

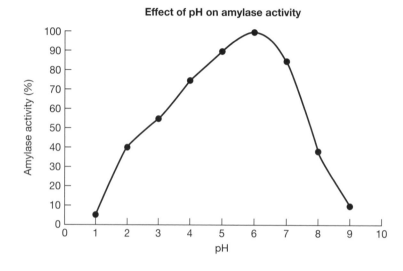

a Describe the pattern of the graph. (2 marks, ★★★)

....

....

b What is the optimum pH of this amylase? (1 mark, ★)

....

c In the investigation, 10 cm³ of starch was used in 120 seconds at pH6. What was the rate of reaction?
(2 marks, ★★★)

NAILIT!

The **optimum pH** is the pH at which the enzyme has the fastest rate of reaction.

Rate of reaction = ...

MATHS SKILLS

Use the formula:

$$\text{Rate of reaction} = \frac{\text{amount of reactant used}}{\text{time}}$$

The heart

(1) **Fill in the missing words below.** (4 marks, ★★)

Blood enters the right side of the heart through the _____ and leaves the

right side of the heart through the _____.

Blood enters the left side of heart through the _____ and leaves the left

side of the heart through the _____.

(2) a **Describe how blood is moved through the right side of the heart.** (3 marks, ★★★)

....

....

....

....

NAILIT!

Include the names of the chambers of the heart, the relevant blood vessels and the names of the valves.

DOIT!

What does the pacemaker in the right atrium control and what happens if it stops working?

b **What is the role of valves in the heart?** (2 marks, ★★)

....

....

(3) **Explain what an artificial pacemaker is and why a person might have one fitted.**
(3 marks, ★★★)

....

....

....

....

The lungs

(1) **Describe how air travels from outside the body to the alveoli.** (3 marks, ★★★)

....

....

....

....

NAILIT!

Include the names of the airways in the lungs: trachea, bronchi and alveoli.

(2) **Match each adaptation of the lung to its purpose.** (3 marks, ★★)

Adaptation of the lung	Purpose
Many alveoli	Gives short diffusion pathway for gases.
Alveolar wall is one cell thick	Keeps the concentration gradient of gases high.
Good supply of blood capillaries	Increase the surface area of the lungs.

DOIT!

Mark the student's answer below using the mark scheme, and suggest how to improve the answer.

Explain why oxygen moves out of the alveoli and into the blood capillary. (3 marks, ★★★★)

There is more oxygen in the alveoli than in the blood capillary. Oxygen moves from the alveoli to the

blood capillary. The blood moves the oxygen away from the alveoli, keeping the concentration of oxygen

in the blood capillary lower than the concentration of oxygen in the alveoli.

MARK SCHEME
The concentration of oxygen in the alveoli is higher than the concentration of oxygen in the blood capillary. (1)

The blood moves the oxygen away from the alveoli, keeping the concentration of oxygen in the blood capillary lower than the concentration of oxygen in the alveoli. (1)

Oxygen diffuses from the alveoli to the blood capillary. (1)

Number of marks for student's answer: ....

How to improve the answer: ....

....

Blood vessels and blood

1 Which of the following statements are true? Tick **one** box. (1 mark, ★★)

A   Arteries have a thin muscular wall.

B   Veins contain valves.

C   Capillary walls are one cell thick.

A and B only	
B and C only	
A, B and C	

2 Blood flows through a 2mm capillary in four seconds. What is the rate of blood flow? (3 marks, ★★★)

....

....

> **MATHS SKILLS**
>
> Use the formula:
>
> $$Rate = \frac{distance}{time}$$

3 Two students are examining the walls of some blood vessels. Student A says that the blood vessel with thick walls must be an artery. Student B says that the blood vessel with the widest lumen must be the artery. State who is correct and explain why arteries have their particular features. (3 marks, ★★★★)

....

....

4 Name **two** components of blood that are not cells. (2 marks, ★)

i   ii   ....

5 Identify the type of blood cells labelled A and B in the image below. (2 marks, ★★★)

A   ....

B   ....

6 What is the function of the following blood cells?

a   **Red blood cells** (1 mark, ★★★)

....

....

b   **White blood cells** (1 mark, ★★★)

....

7 Describe how white blood cells are adapted for their function. (3 marks, ★★★★)

....

....

....

> **NAILIT!**
>
> Include one adaptation of phagocytes, neutrophils and lymphocytes in your answer.

Coronary heart disease

(1) **What type of disease is coronary heart disease (CHD)?** (1 mark, ★)

....

(2) **Describe how CHD develops.** (2 marks, ★★★)

....

....

(3) **Match each symptom of CHD to the correct description.** (3 marks, ★★)

Symptom	Description
Angina	Muscle weakness in the heart or a faulty valve.
Heart failure	Chest pains due to restricted blood flow to heart muscle.
Heart attack	The blood supply to the heart muscle is suddenly blocked.

(4) **Name two treatments for CHD. For each, state one advantage and one disadvantage.** (4 marks, ★★★★)

1   Treatment: ....

Advantage: ....

Disadvantage: ....

2   Treatment: ....

Advantage: ....

Disadvantage: ....

DO IT!

In this topic you may be asked to evaluate different methods of treatment, considering the advantages and disadvantages of each.

Here are six treatments for CHD. What are the advantages and disadvantages for each?

stents, statins, mechanical valve replacement, biological valve replacement, heart

transplant, artificial heart (temporary)

Health issues and effect of lifestyle

(1) **What is a communicable disease?** (1 mark, ★)

....

(2) **Name two communicable diseases.** (2 marks, ★)

i .... ii ....

(3) **Describe two health conditions that can interact.** (2 marks, ★★★)

....

....

(4) **The graph below shows the number of deaths per 100 000 population from cardiovascular disease (CVD) in Australia in 2012.**

Deaths per 100 000 population

Describe the pattern in the graph.

(2 marks, ★★★)

....

....

> **NAILIT!**
>
> When asked to **describe** a graph, you are not being asked to **explain** the reasons for a pattern/correlation, just what the pattern/correlation is.

(5) **What is a non-communicable disease?** (1 mark, ★)

....

(6) **A doctor sees a patient for a check-up and asks about the person's lifestyle. The patient smokes, drinks some alcohol each week, and does little exercise. What advice could the doctor give about possible health risks of this lifestyle?** (3 marks, ★★★)

....

....

....

(7) **Describe the human and financial costs of non-communicable diseases.** (3 marks, ★★★★)

....

....

....

....

> **NAILIT!**
>
> Think about the changes that people would have to make and the cost of things they might have to do because of their illness.

Cancer

(1) **Name some of the risk factors associated with cancer.** (2 marks, ★)

....

....

(2) **Describe how normal cells can become cancerous.** (3 marks, ★★★)

NAILIT!

Include the word **mutation** in your answer.

....

....

....

....

(3) **Name and compare the two types of tumour.** (3 marks, ★★★★)

....

....

....

....

....

....

NAILIT!

Compare similarities and differences between the two types of tumour.

(4) **The graph shows the number of cases of breast cancer in women and the number of deaths per 100 000 population in the UK, before and after screening was introduced in 1987.**

Describe patterns on the graph and suggest reasons for them. (4 marks, ★★★★★)

....

....

....

....

....

....

....

....

Plant tissues

(1) Match each plant tissue to its function. (4 marks, ★★)

Plant tissue

Spongy mesophyll

Palisade tissue

Xylem

Phloem

Function

The main site of photosynthesis in a leaf.

Transport of sugar sap around the plant.

Site of gas exchange in the leaf.

Transport of water to the leaf.

(2) Describe how palisade cells are adapted to their function. (2 marks, ★★★)

....

....

(3) The drawing below shows a transverse section through a leaf.

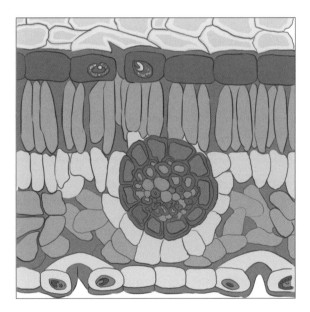

Label the following:

- a spongy mesophyll cell (1 mark, ★★)
- a palisade cell (1 mark, ★★)
- the xylem. (1 mark, ★★)

NAILIT!

Palisade cells are found at the top of the leaf where there is more sunlight.

Transpiration and translocation

(1) a **Name the apparatus used to measure the rate of transpiration.** (1 mark, ★)

....

b **In a transpiration experiment, 20 cm³ of water was lost in five hours.**

Calculate the rate of transpiration. Show your working. (2 marks, ★★★)

> **NAILIT!**
>
> Use the formula:
>
> $$\text{Rate} = \frac{\text{volume of water}}{\text{time}}$$

Rate of transpiration = ...

(2) **Describe and explain how guard cells control the loss of water from the leaf.** (3 marks, ★★★★)

> **NAILIT!**
>
> Include how the guard cells change shape in your answer.

....

....

....

....

(3) **What is the difference between transpiration and translocation?** (4 marks, ★★★★)

....

....

....

....

....

(4) **Xerophytes are specialised plants that can live in habitats with very little water. Describe two adaptations of xerophytes and explain how they help the plant to survive.** (4 marks, ★★★★)

....

....

....

....

....

Infection and response

Communicable (infectious) diseases

(1) **What is a pathogen?** (1 mark, ★)

....

(2) **Match each disease to the pathogen that causes it.** (3 marks, ★★)

Disease	Pathogen
Tuberculosis	Bacterium
	Virus
Malaria	Fungus
Athlete's foot	Protist

(3) **Compare the lytic and lysogenic lifecycles of viruses.** (3 marks, ★★★)

....

....

....

(4) **The number of cases of HIV among intravenous drug users (IDUs) in Finland is shown in the graph below. A needle exchange programme was introduced in 1999.**

> **NAILIT!**
>
> Make sure that you describe each stage of the graph and use numbers (from the graph) to justify your explanation.

Use evidence from the graph to describe and explain the pattern of HIV cases among intravenous drug users from 1999. (3 marks, ★★★★)

....

....

....

....

Viral and bacterial diseases

(1) **Describe the symptoms of measles.** (2 marks, ★★★)

....

(2) a **What is tobacco mosaic virus (TMV)?** (2 marks, ★)

....

....

b **Explain why plants with TMV carry out less photosynthesis than plants that do not have TMV.** (2 marks, ★★★)

....

....

(3) **During the First World War, many soldiers living in trenches caught influenza. At the end of the war, a global influenza pandemic killed more than 20 million people worldwide. Describe and explain how this virus could have infected so many people.** (4 marks, ★★★★)

....

....

....

....

NAILIT!

Recall how viruses are transmitted from person to person.

(4) a **What are the symptoms of salmonella poisoning?** (2 marks, ★)

....

b **Describe how severe cases of salmonella poisoning are treated.** (2 marks, ★★)

....

....

(5) a **Antibiotics are often used to treat gonorrhoea infections. Recently, some strains of bacteria that cause gonorrhoea have become resistant to antibiotics. Explain what this means.** (2 marks, ★★★★)

....

....

NAILIT!

A strain is a sub-group of a species of bacterium.

b **The number of cases of gonorrhoea infection in the UK increased by 11 % from 2014 to 2015. Suggest what may have caused this increase.** (1 mark, ★★★★)

....

Fungal and protist diseases

1 a **Fill in the missing words.** (3 marks, ★★)

Rose black spot is a .... disease that affects roses. The leaves

of the rose are covered with .... This reduces the rate of

.... in the leaves.

b **Describe how rose black spot is treated.** (2 marks, ★★)

....

....

2 a **Malaria is spread by mosquitoes. List some ways of preventing malaria infection in areas where there are mosquitoes.** (3 marks, ★★)

....

....

....

b **A group of scientists studying malaria found that there were more cases of malaria in areas with shallow pools of water. Describe and explain how they could use this knowledge to reduce the spread of malaria.** (2 marks, ★★★★)

....

....

....

NAILIT!

Topic link: Mosquitoes are part of a food chain. The food chain will be disrupted if the mosquitoes are removed.

STRETCHIT!

Can you find out which species populations would be affected by mass mosquito removal?

3 **Ash dieback is a fungal disease that could cause the extinction of ash trees in the UK. Suggest two ways that this could be prevented.** (2 marks, ★★★)

i ....

ii ....

Human defence systems

(1) Match each body part to the non-specific defence. (4 marks, ★★)

Body part	Defence
Skin	Cilia move mucus up to the throat.
Nose	Contain lysozymes which kill bacteria.
Trachea	Hydrochloric acid and proteases kill pathogens.
Stomach	Physical barrier against pathogens.
Tears	Small hairs and mucus trap airborne particles.

(2) a Name two types of white blood cell that kill pathogens. (2 marks, ★)

i ....

ii ....

b Describe how white blood cells attack a specific pathogen. (5 marks, ★★★)

....

....

....

....

....

NAILIT!

Discuss the action of antibodies in your answer.

WORKIT!

Describe and explain the body's defence against the influenza virus. (4 marks, ★★★)

The influenza virus cannot pass through the skin, which is a non-specific barrier. (1)

Mucus traps any inhaled virus, which is then moved up to the throat by cilia. (1)

Phagocytes will engulf the virus by phagocytosis. (1)

Lymphoctyes will produce antibodies against the virus. (1)

Vaccination

1. **Fill in the missing words.** (3 marks, ★★)

   Vaccines contain a dead or an .... form of a ....

   Vaccines are injected into the body where they stimulate the ....

2. **Describe and explain how a vaccine works.** (4 marks, ★★★★)

   ....

   ....

   ....

   ....

   ....

   ....

   NAILIT!

   Remember to include antibodies in your answer.

3. **Give one advantage and one disadvantage of vaccination programs.** (2 marks, ★★★)

   ....

   ....

   ....

DOIT!

Mark the student's answer below using the mark scheme, and suggest how to improve the answer.

> Vaccination programmes are used worldwide. Explain how this helps to eradicate disease. (3 marks, ★★★)
>
> If enough people in a country are vaccinated against a disease, the disease cannot be passed from
>
> infected people, as the people around the infected person have been vaccinated.

MARK SCHEME
If enough people in a country are vaccinated against a pathogen, the pathogen cannot be transmitted from infected people, (1) as the people around the infected person have been vaccinated. (1) This is called herd immunity. (1)

Number of marks for student's answer: ....

How to improve the answer: ....

....

....

Antibiotics and painkillers

(1) **Give an example of an antibiotic and an example of a painkiller.** (2 marks, ★)

Antibiotic .... Painkiller ....

(2) **Describe how antibiotics work.** (2 marks, ★★★)

....

....

(3) **Antiviral drugs are used to treat viral infections. Explain why antiviral drugs are not always effective.** (2 marks, ★★★★)

....

....

(4) **The graph below shows the effectiveness of two painkillers. What is the advantage of using each painkiller?** (2 marks, ★★★★★)

....

....

....

....

....

....

....

....

(5) **Some strains of bacteria are becoming resistant to some antibiotics. Suggest how antibiotic resistance could be reduced.** (3 marks, ★★★★)

....

....

....

....

New drugs

(1) Match each drug to the plant or microorganism that it was discovered in. (3 marks, ★★)

Drug	Plant or microorganism
Aspirin	*Penicillium*
Digitalis	Willow bark
Penicillin	Foxgloves

(2) How are new drugs discovered? (2 marks, ★★★)

....

....

(3) A new painkiller is being developed. Describe how the new painkiller is tested to make sure it is safe for patients to take. Explain the purpose of each step. (4 marks, ★★★★)

....

....

....

NAILIT!

Make sure you describe preclinical and clinical trials.

....

....

....

DOIT!

Topic link: How does the maintenance of biodiversity affect the discovery or development of new drugs?

WORKIT!

The results of a clinical trial are peer reviewed before publication. What is a peer review? (1 mark, ★★)

When the results of a clinical trial are reviewed/judged by other scientists. (1)

Monoclonal antibodies and their uses

(1) **What type of cells make monoclonal antibodies?** (1 mark, ★)

....

(2) **Describe how monoclonal antibodies work.**
(2 marks, ★★★)

....

....

> **NAILIT!**
> Recall that antibodies are complementary in shape to their antigen.

(3) **A scientist wants to make large amounts of monoclonal antibody specific to a particular antigen. Explain how these can be made using mouse lymphocytes.** (5 marks, ★★★★)

....

....

....

....

....

(4) **Give two uses of monoclonal antibodies.** (2 marks, ★)

i .... ii ....

(5) **What are the possible side effects of using monoclonal antibodies to treat diseases?**
(2 marks, ★★★)

....

....

(6) **Describe the advantages and disadvantages of using monoclonal antibodies to treat diseases. Include the idea of specificity in your answer.** (3 marks, ★★★★★)

....

....

....

> **NAILIT!**
> Think about any ethical issues of how monoclonal antibodies are made.

....

....

Plant diseases and defences

(1) **What is chlorosis and what is it caused by?** (2 marks, ★)

....

(2) **Which one of the following statements is not true? Tick one box.** (1 mark, ★★)

Rose black spot causes stunted growth.	
Aphids are pests that cause malformed stems.	
Tobacco mosaic virus causes discolouration of the leaves.	

(3) **How can you identify a plant disease?** (2 marks, ★★★)

....

....

(4) **A gardener is examining plants in a greenhouse and notices that some have a nitrate deficiency.**

a **How does the gardener know that the plants have nitrate deficiency?** (2 marks, ★★★)

....

b **Explain why plants needs nitrates.** (2 marks, ★★★★)

....

....

> **NAILIT!**
>
> Think about which biological molecules contain nitrogen.

(5) **Name two physical plant defences.** (2 marks, ★)

i ....   ii ....

(6) **Describe a chemical plant adaptation and how it protects the plant.** (2 marks, ★★★)

....

(7) **The image below shows a branch of a pine tree.**

What mechanical adaptations shown in the image does this plant have to ensure its survival? Explain the purpose of each mechanical adaptation. (4 marks, ★★★★)

....

....

....

> **NAILIT!**
>
> Mechanical adaptations alter the plant's structure.

Photosynthesis

(1) a **Write the word equation for photosynthesis.** (2 marks, ★)

....

b **What type of reaction is photosynthesis?** (1 mark, ★)

....

c **Explain the use of carbon dioxide in photosynthesis.** (2 marks, ★★★★)

> **NAILIT!**
>
> It is the type of reaction that takes in more heat than it gives off.

....

....

d **A student wants to measure the rate of photosynthesis in a plant at different temperatures. Plan an investigation to do this.** (4 marks, ★★★★)

....

....

....

....

....

....

....

....

Rate of photosynthesis

(1) **Name a factor that increases the rate of photosynthesis.** (1 mark, ★)

....

(2) **a What is a limiting factor?** (2 marks, ★)

....

....

b Which of these graphs shows the rate of photosynthesis at increasing light intensity?
(1 mark, ★★★)

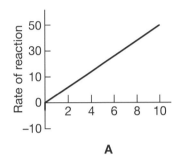
A

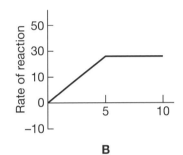
B

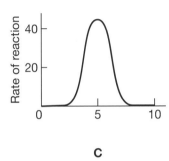
C

....

(3) **The rate of photosynthesis is calculated by measuring the volume of oxygen that a plant gives off in a given time.**

A plant gives off 24 cm³ of oxygen in four minutes. Calculate the rate of photosynthesis. Show your working. (3 marks, ★★★)

NAILIT!

Use the formula:

$$\text{Rate} = \frac{\text{volume of product released}}{\text{time}}$$

Rate of photosynthesis = ...

Investigating the effect of light intensity on the rate of photosynthesis

(1) **Some students investigate the rate of photosynthesis in pondweed at different intensities of light. The students placed a lamp at different distances from the pondweed and measured the volume of oxygen given off after five minutes.**

a **Name the independent and dependent variables in this investigation.** (2 marks, ★★)

Independent variable ....

Dependent variable ....

b **Describe what the students could have done to make sure that this investigation is valid.** (3 marks, ★★★)

....

....

....

NAILIT!

Think about the variables that need to be kept the same – these are called the **control variables**.

MATHS SKILLS

$$\text{Rate} = \frac{\text{volume of product released}}{\text{time}}$$

c **Students recorded the volume of oxygen released in five minutes. The table shows their results.**

Distance of lamp from plant (cm)	Volume of oxygen released (cm³)	Time (min)	Rate of photosynthesis (cm³/min)
0	200	5	40
25	195	5	
50	85	5	
75	40	5	
100	10	5	

Calculate the rate of photosynthesis of the plants for each distance from the lamp and complete the table. (4 marks, ★★★)

d **Explain why the rate of photosynthesis decreases as the light is moved further from the pondweed.** (1 mark, ★★★)

....

....

Uses of glucose

(1) **Name two uses of glucose in plants.** (2 marks, ★)

i ....

ii ....

NAILIT!

Glucose is used in plants to make substances.

(2) **Which statement is true? Tick one box.** (1 mark, ★★)

Glucose is a lipid.	
Glucose has the chemical formula $C_6H_{12}O_6$.	
Animals need glucose to make starch.	

(3) **How do plants make glucose?** (1 mark, ★★★)

....

....

....

NAILIT!

Glucose is the product of a reaction.

DOIT!

Mark the student's answer below using the mark scheme, and suggest how to improve the answer.

Explain why glucose is important in animals. (3 marks, ★★★)

Glucose is needed for respiration to release energy, and is converted into glycogen for storage.

MARK SCHEME

Needed for respiration to release energy. (1)

Converted into glycogen for storage. (1)

Used to produce fat for storage. (1)

Number of marks for student's answer: ....

How to improve the answer: ....

....

....

Respiration and metabolism

(1) a **What is the word equation for aerobic respiration?** (1 mark, ★)

....

b **What type of reaction is respiration?** (1 mark, ★)

....

NAILIT!

Does respiration release more heat than it takes in?

(2) a **Where in the cell does aerobic respiration take place?** (1 mark, ★)

....

b **What is the chemical equation for aerobic respiration?** (2 marks, ★★★)

....

(3) **Describe what happens in muscle cells during anaerobic respiration.** (3 marks, ★★★)

....

....

....

(4) **A group of students wanted to measure the rate of respiration in yeast. Describe a method that they could use.** (3 marks, ★★★)

....

....

....

....

(5) **Describe some metabolic reactions that happen in the body.** (2 marks, ★★★)

....

....

(6) **Explain why metabolic reactions need energy.** (2 marks, ★★★★)

....

....

NAILIT!

The amount of energy stored in food can be calculated using calorimetry, this measures the energy transferred when food is burned and heats up water.

Response to exercise

1 a **Describe how to measure a person's pulse rate after exercise.** (3 marks, ★★★)

....

....

....

....

....

> **NAILIT!**
>
> The pulse is found in the **arteries** of the body.

b **If a person's pulse is measured as 18 pulses in 15 seconds, what is the pulse rate in beats per minute?** (1 mark, ★★★)

....

....

> **MATHS SKILLS**
>
> To calculate the beats per minute from the number of pulses in 15 seconds, multiply the number by four.

2 a **Describe and explain two effects of exercise on the human body.** (4 marks, ★★★★)

....

....

....

b **An athlete's stroke volume is 80 cm^3 and heart rate is 60 beats per minute. Calculate the cardiac output.** (2 marks, ★★★)

....

....

....

....

> **NAILIT!**
>
> Cardiac output = stroke volume × heart rate
> Check if your exam board requires you to know this calculation.

3 **Marley runs a 100 m race in 12.8 seconds but his breathing rate remains high for several minutes after he has finished, even though he has sat down to rest. Explain why his breathing rate does not return to normal straight away at the end of the race.**
(4 marks, ★★★★)

....

....

....

Homeostasis

(1) **Complete the following sentence about homeostasis.** (3 marks, ★)

Homeostasis keeps all the .... conditions of the body

.... whatever the .... conditions might be.

(2) a **Controlling the levels of blood sugar is one example of homeostasis. Name two other examples of homeostasis.** (2 marks, ★)

....

....

b **Describe how homeostasis controls the blood sugar levels in the body.** (5 marks, ★★★★)

....

....

....

....

....

....

NAILIT!

You need to include what happens when blood sugar levels are high and when they are low, so make sure you mention insulin *and* glucagon in your answer. Thinking about how diabetics treat 'hypos' and 'hypers' might help you to remember.

(3) **What is the role of the brain in homeostasis?** (3 marks, ★★★)

....

....

....

WORKIT!

Explain why it is important to maintain an internal body temperature of 37°C. (4 marks, ★★★)

Enzymes are needed to carry out reactions in the body. (1)

Enzymes have an optimum temperature of 37°C. (1)

If the temperature is too low, the enzymes will not react quickly enough to maintain life. (1)

If the temperature is too high, the enzymes will denature, and no longer be able to carry out their function. (1)

The human nervous system and reflexes

(1) **Which one of the following statements is true? Tick one box.** (1 mark, ★★)

A	The peripheral nervous system is made of the brain and the spinal cord.	
B	Sensory neurones detect stimuli and send nerve impulses to the brain.	
C	Motor neurones receive nerve impulses from the brain.	
D	The brain is an effector and responds to the stimuli.	

(2) a **Put the terms receptor, response, coordinator and stimulus into the correct order.** (4 marks, ★★)

.... $\longrightarrow$ .... $\longrightarrow$ .... $\longrightarrow$ effector $\longrightarrow$ ....

b **Describe the role of the coordinator.** (2 marks, ★★)

....

(3) **A person is testing their reaction time by pressing a button when a light appears on a screen. Describe and explain the action of the nervous system when the light appears on the screen.** (4 marks, ★★★)

....

....

....

(4) **Name two neurones involved in a reflex arc.** (2 marks, ★)

i .... ii ....

(5) **Compare the structure and function of the three different neurones found in a reflex arc.** (3 marks, ★★)

....

....

....

....

NAILIT!

You may be asked to compare the different types of neurons in the exam. You need to know:

- the physical differences
- the functions of each type
- the order they perform in a reflex arc.

(6) a **Compare reflexes and voluntary reactions.** (2 marks, ★★)

....

....

b **Explain why reflex actions are important.** (2 marks, ★★)

....

....

Investigating the effect of a factor on human reaction time

(1) **A student decided to measure their reaction time before and after drinking caffeine. Here is their method.**

Measure reaction time by timing how long it takes them to press a button when they see a light on a screen.

Drink a cup of cola.

Measure reaction time again.

a **Describe how you could alter the method to make it more valid and reliable.** (4 marks, ★★★)

....

....

....

....

> **NAILIT!**
>
> - The **independent variable** is the one which you deliberately change (in order to observe its effects on the dependent variable).
>
> - The **dependent variable** is the one which may change as a result of changes to the independent variable.
>
> - All other variables must be controlled to make the experiment a 'fair test'. These are called the **control variables**.
>
> - The **independent** variable always goes in the left-hand column of a results table and on the horizontal axis (x-axis) of a results graph.

b **The student found the reaction times before drinking cola were 0.55, 0.45 and 0.50 seconds; and 0.40, 0.35 and 0.3 seconds after drinking cola. Record this data in a table.** (3 marks, ★★★)

c **Calculate the means and add them to the table.** (2 marks, ★★)

The brain and the eye

(1) **Label the areas of the brain.** (3 marks, ★★)

A ....

B ....

C ....

(2) **What is the function of the following parts of the brain?**

a **Cerebellum** (2 marks, ★★)

....

b **Cerebral cortex** (2 marks, ★★)

....

(3) **How have neuroscientists been able to map regions of the brain to particular functions?**
(2 marks, ★★)

....

(4) **Label these sections of the eye.** (4 marks, ★★)

A ....

B ....

C ....

D ....

Sclera

Vitreous

(5) a **What is the function of A?** (1 mark, ★★)

....

b **Explain why the function of A is important.** (2 marks, ★★★)

....

....

Focusing the eye

(1) a **What does accommodation of the eye mean?** (1 mark, ★★)

....

....

b **Explain what happens in the eye when looking at a near object.** (3 marks, ★★★)

....

....

....

NAILIT!

You will need to learn the correct names for long- and short-sightedness:

- Myopia (short-sightedness)
- Hyperopia (long-sightedness).

c i **Describe what happens in the eye of a person with myopia.** (2 marks, ★★★)

....

....

ii **What type of lens would correct myopia?** (1 mark, ★)

....

iii **Explain how this lens works.** (2 marks, ★★)

....

....

iv **Describe how colour blindness affects vision.** (1 mark, ★★)

....

....

d **Describe how cataracts affect a person's vision.** (2 marks, ★★★)

....

....

....

Control of body temperature

(1) **Name two ways in which the body warms itself up when it is too cold.** (2 marks, ★)

i ....

ii ....

(2) **Suggest possible symptoms of hypothermia.** (2 marks, ★★)

....

....

(3) **Describe how body temperature is monitored and regulated.** (5 marks, ★★★★)

....

....

....

....

....

....

....

NAILIT!

The key words in Q3 are *monitored* and *regulated* – you will be expected to include the **thermoregulatory centre** in your answer.

DO IT!

Mark the student's answer below using the mark scheme, and suggest how to improve the answer.

A man goes out on a sunny day without a hat. Soon he begins to feel sick and dizzy. Suggest why and give advice on what the man should do. (3 marks, ★★)

The man is suffering from heatstroke. He should sit in the shade and drink some water to cool down.

MARK SCHEME
The man is suffering from heatstroke/hyperthermia (1). He should keep himself cool by sitting in the shade. (1) He should rehydrate by drinking some water. (1)

Number of marks for student's answer: ....

How to improve the answer: ....

....

Human endocrine system

(1) **Match the glands of the endocrine system with their hormones.** (4 marks, ★★)

Gland	Hormones
Pituitary gland	Insulin and glucagon
Pancreas	Growth hormone, FSH and LH
Thyroid	Testosterone
	Thyroxine
Ovary	Progesterone and oestrogen

(2) **How is the endocrine system controlled?** (2 marks, ★★★)

....

....

....

(3) **Compare the properties of the endocrine system and the nervous system.** (4 marks, ★★★)

....

....

....

....

....

NAILIT!

Think about the speed and lasting effects of each system.

Control of blood glucose concentration

(1) **Where in the body are insulin and glucagon produced?** (1 mark, ★)

....

(2) **Describe the effects of insulin on the body.** (3 marks, ★★)

....

....

....

(3) **Glucagon is released when the blood sugar levels are low. Explain how glucagon returns the blood glucose level back to normal.** (3 marks, ★★★)

....

....

....

....

(4) **Suggest what could happen in the body if insulin is not released.** (2 marks, ★★)

....

....

....

NAILIT!

Think about what happens to the body if it does not take up sugar – for example, when a diabetic person experiences hyperglycaemia.

DOIT!

Each of the following are part of every control system. Make sure you can write a definition for each:

• receptor
• coordination centre
• effector.

What are the receptors, coordination centre and effectors involved in the control of blood glucose?

Diabetes

(1) **What is diabetes?** (2 marks, ★★)

....

....

(2) **What is hyperglycaemia?** (1 mark, ★)

....

(3) **Compare and contrast type 1 and type 2 diabetes.** (4 marks, ★★★)

....

....

....

....

....

....

NAILIT!

Compare what is happening inside the body, the causes and the treatment.

(4) **Describe what happens to the blood sugar levels of people with diabetes after a meal.** (2 marks, ★★★)

....

....

....

DOIT!

Mark the student's answer below using the mark scheme, and suggest how to improve the answer.

Student A says that all people with diabetes inject insulin. Student B says that only people with type 1 diabetes inject insulin. Who is correct and why? (3 marks, ★★★)

Student B is correct. People with type 1 diabetes need to inject insulin because they don't have any.

MARK SCHEME
Student B is correct. (1) People with type 1 diabetes do not produce any/enough insulin. (1) They need to inject insulin so that cells and the liver can take up glucose after a meal. (1)

Number of marks for student's answer: ....

How to improve the answer: ....

....

Maintaining water and nitrogen balance in the body

(1) a **What is osmosis?** (1 mark, ★)

....

b **What is the effect on animal cells if the fluid around the cells is more concentrated than inside the cell?** (2 marks, ★★)

....

....

(2) **Describe how glucose moves from the blood into the nephron and back into the blood.** (4 marks, ★★★)

....

....

....

(3) **Label the parts of the kidney below.** (3 marks, ★★)

Nephrons in cortex

Renal artery and vein

(4) **State the role of ADH.** (2 marks, ★★)

....

....

(5) **Describe the role of the brain in controlling water levels in the body.** (4 marks, ★★)

....

....

....

(6) **A person doesn't have a drink for a few hours. Explain how ADH helps to maintain the water content of the blood.** (3 marks, ★★★)

....

....

....

....

NAILIT!

Remember to relate the permeability of the collecting ducts in the kidney to the level of ADH so that you get all the marks for this question.

Dialysis

(1) **Describe how a dialysis machine works.** (4 marks, ★★★)

....

....

....

....

....

....

....

NAILIT!

Include the terms **dialysate**, and **partially permeable membrane**.

(2) **Evaluate the advantages and disadvantages of having dialysis or a kidney transplant.**
(4 marks, ★★★)

....

....

....

....

....

....

....

NAILIT!

Think about the amount of time people spend on dialysis.

(3) **High potassium levels in the blood are dangerous. Orange juice contains a lot of potassium. Suggest why people on dialysis are advised not to drink orange juice.**
(3 marks, ★★★)

....

....

....

Hormones in human reproduction

1. **Match the hormone to the endocrine gland where it is made.** (3 marks, ★)

Hormone	Endocrine gland
Testosterone	Ovaries
Oestrogen	Pituitary gland
Follicle-stimulating hormone	Testes

2. a **What is the role of follicle-stimulating hormone (FSH)?** (1 mark, ★)

....

b **Which hormone stimulates the release of LH?** (1 mark, ★)

....

3. **The graph below shows hormone levels during the menstrual cycle.**

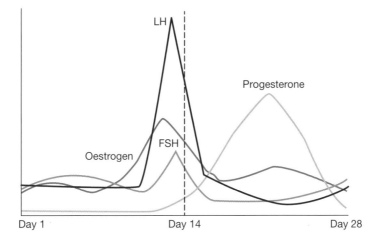

a **What happens when luteinising hormone (LH) peaks just before day 14?** (1 mark, ★★)

....

b **What effect does progesterone have on the uterus after day 14? Explain why this is important if the egg is fertilised.** (2 marks, ★★)

....

....

....

Contraception

(1) **Match the non-hormonal methods of contraception to how they work.** (3 marks, ★)

Condoms		Kill sperm
Intrauterine device (IUD)		Prevents implantation of an embryo
Spermicidal agents		Trap sperm

(2) a **Name two examples of hormonal contraception.** (2 marks, ★)

i ....

ii ....

b **Explain how hormonal contraceptives work.** (3 marks, ★★★)

....

....

....

NAILIT!

Think about the hormones that are in different types of hormonal contraceptives. Don't forget to include the effects of progesterone in your answer.

(3) **Compare the effectiveness of hormonal and non-hormonal methods of contraception.** (4 marks, ★★★★)

....

....

....

....

....

....

Using hormones to treat infertility

(1) **Which of the following statements are true? Tick one box.** (1 mark, ★)

A   IVF is a type of fertilisation that happens outside of the body.

B   FSH and oestrogen are given to the woman before IVF.

C   Several eggs are usually fertilised by IVF at the same time.

i	A and B only	
ii	B and C only	
iii	A and C only	

(2) **Describe the IVF procedure.** (3 marks, ★★)

....

....

....

(3) **Explain the advantages and disadvantages of using IVF.** (4 marks, ★★★)

....

....

....

....

....

DO IT!

Mark the student's answer below using the mark scheme, and suggest how to improve the answer.

Describe how hormones are used in infertility treatment. (2 marks, ★★★)

Follicle-stimulating hormone and luteinising hormone are given to increase the number of eggs.

MARK SCHEME
Follicle-stimulating hormone is used to increase the number of eggs (1) and luteinising hormone is given to release the eggs/stimulate ovulation. (1)

Number of marks for student's answer: ....

How to improve the answer: ....

....

Negative feedback

① **What is negative feedback?** (2 marks, ★)

....

....

② a **Where in the body is adrenaline produced?** (1 mark, ★)

....

b **Which of the following is an effect of adrenaline? Tick one box.** (1 mark, ★)

A, B and C only	
B, C and D only	
A, B and D only	
A, C and D only	

A Heart rate increases.

B Breathing rate increases.

C More blood flows to the skin and intestines.

D Stimulates the liver to release glucose from glycogen.

③ **The diagram shows how the level of thyroxine in the body is maintained by thyroid releasing hormone (TRH) and thyroid stimulating hormone (TSH).**

Use information from the diagram to explain how thyroxine levels are maintained.

(3 marks, ★★★★)

....

....

....

....

....

....

....

NAIL IT!

Don't forget that thyroxine is a hormone controlled by a **negative feedback** cycle. When answering questions about the action of the hormones which regulate thyroxine, remember to mention it is the **levels of thyroxine** (high or low) which stimulate the hypothalamus actions.

Plant hormones

(1) **Match the tropism to the factor it responds to.** (3 marks, ★)

Tropism	Responding to
Phototropism	Gravity
Geotropism	Light
Hydrotropism	Water

(2) **Describe the role of auxin in phototropism.** (4 marks, ★★★)

....

....

....

....

(3) **Explain why a shoot grows upwards and a root grows downwards even if the seed is upside down.** (4 marks, ★★★★)

....

....

....

....

NAILIT!

Include the distribution of auxin in the cells of the root and shoot in your answer to Q3.

(4) **Give one effect each of gibberellins and ethene on plants.** (2 marks, ★)

....

....

Investigating the effect of light or gravity on the growth of newly germinated seedlings

(1) **Some students have investigated the effect of light on germinated seedlings. They have recorded their findings in the table below.**

Day	Position of light	Length of shoot	Direction of growth
1	Left	2	Left
2	Right	3.5	Right
3	Left	4.1	Left
4	Right	5.2	Right
5	Left	5.8	Left

a **Identify a mistake in the table and correct it.**

Mistake .... (1 mark, ★★)

Correction .... (1 mark, ★★)

(2) **Name two variables that need to be kept the same in this investigation.** (2 marks, ★★)

....

....

(3) **Use your knowledge of plant hormones to explain these results.** (3 marks, ★★★)

....

....

....

....

....

NAILIT!

Describe the effect of auxin build-up in the shoots due to the direction of the light.

(4) **Which of the following plant hormones are appropriate for each use?** (2 marks, ★★)

A – Gibberellins

B – Auxins

- weedkiller ....
- rooting powder ....
- to end seed dormancy ....

- to promote flowering ....
- to promote growth in tissue culturing

....
- to increase fruit size ....

Inheritance, variation and evolution

Sexual and asexual reproduction

1   **a**   **Name the male and female gametes in animals.** (2 marks, ★)

Female ....

Male ....

  b   **What is the process that produces gametes?** (1 mark, ★)

....

2   **Match the organism with the type of asexual reproduction they use.** (4 marks, ★★)

Organism	**Asexual reproduction**
Bacteria	Runners
Yeast	Budding
Strawberry plants	Binary fission
Potatoes	Tubers

3   **Malarial parasites reproduce sexually in mosquito hosts and asexually in human hosts. Explain the advantages of this to the malarial parasites.** (4 marks, ★★★)

....

....

....

....

....

NAILIT!

Include ideas about genetic variation and natural selection.

Meiosis

(1) **Complete the table.** (3 marks, ★★)

	Mitosis	Meiosis
Number of daughter cells	2	
Number of chromosomes	Full	
Genetically identical		No

(2) **Describe what happens during meiosis.** (3 marks, ★★★)

....

....

....

....

(3) **What happens during fertilisation?** (3 marks, ★★★)

....

....

....

....

DOIT!

Mark the student's answer below using the mark scheme, and suggest how to improve the answer.

Explain why meiosis is important in variation. (3 marks, ★★★★)

Meiosis makes sex cells that are genetically different. This means that when male and female sex cells

fuse, there is a wide possibility of different alleles.

MARK SCHEME
Meiosis makes genetically different sex cells. (1) During fertilisation, there are many different possible combinations of alleles, (1) resulting in a wide variation of genotypes in a population. (1)

Number of marks for student's answer: ....

How to improve the answer: ....

....

DNA and the genome

1 **Which of the following statements are true? Tick one box.** (1 mark, ★★)

A   DNA is found in the nucleus of the cell.

B   Each gene contains a code to make a specific protein.

C   Many genes are folded into large structures called chromatin.

D   DNA is made of two stands that form a double helix.

i	A, C and D only.
ii	A, B, and C only.
iii	A, B, and D only.
iv	B, C, and D only.

2 **a How many chromosomes are there in human body cells?** (1 mark, ★)

....

b If an organism has 38 chromosomes in the body cells, how many chromosomes will there be in the gametes? (1 mark, ★)

....

3 **Explain why studying the human genome is useful in medicine and science.** (3 marks, ★★★)

....

....

....

....

> **NAILIT!**
>
> Consider why this might be important for the study of diseases, treatments and human migration.

4 **Two students extracted DNA from a banana using the following method.**

1.   Crush the banana in a beaker containing soap and water.

2.   Filtered the crushed banana into a test tube.

3.   Added ice-cold ethanol to the test tube.

4.   The DNA was carefully removed from the ethanol using a glass rod.

Explain the purpose of steps 1 and 3. (3 marks, ★★★★)

....

....

....

....

DNA structure

(1) a **Draw and label a DNA nucleotide.** (3 marks, ★★)

NAILIT!

There are three parts to a nucleotide.

b **What is a chain of nucleotides called?** (1 mark, ★)

....

(2) **Describe how the bases in DNA form base pairs.** (3 marks, ★★)

....

....

....

(3) **Explain how the sequence of amino acids in a polypeptide is controlled by the DNA sequence.** (3 marks, ★★★)

....

....

....

....

....

....

DOIT!

Learn which bases pair with each other and how. Can you think of a way to remember the pairings? For example:

Territorial **A**rmy

George **C**ross

NAILIT!

Make sure you understand how a change in DNA structure may result in a change in the protein synthesised by a gene.

However, you do **not** need to know the detailed chemical structure of amino acids, proteins, mRNA or tRNA.

Protein synthesis

(1) **Put the stages of protein synthesis into the correct order.** (4 marks, ★★★)

A   The ribosome translates the code on the mRNA, three bases at a time.

B   The protein breaks away from the ribosome and folds into its shape.

C   The DNA code of the gene is transcribed into a messenger RNA code.

D   The three bases control which amino acid the transfer RNA will add onto the protein next.

E   Carrier molecules called transfer RNA bring the amino acids to the ribosome.

F   The mRNA leaves the nucleus and finds a ribosome.

....F....   ....B....

(2) **Describe how a protein folds.** (2 marks, ★★)

....

....

....

....

(3) **Substitution mutations have occurred in the coding and the non-coding part of the DNA. Explain the effects of these mutations in the following.**

a **The coding part of DNA.** (3 marks, ★★★)

....

....

....

....

b **The non-coding part of DNA.** (2 marks, ★★★)

....

....

....

Genetic inheritance

1. **Match the genetics keywords to their meaning.** (4 marks, ★)

| Homozygous | The alleles that are present in the genome. |

Homozygous

Heterozygous

Genotype

Phenotype

The alleles that are present in the genome.

When two different alleles are present.

An allele that is always expressed.

When two copies of the same allele are present.

The characteristics that are expressed by those alleles.

2. **A mouse with black fur and a mouse with brown fur had offspring. The black mouse has the genotype, Bb. Mice with brown fur always have the genotype, bb.**

   a **Draw a Punnett square to show the genotypes.** (2 marks, ★★★)

   b **What are the possible phenotypes of the offspring?** (1 mark, ★★★)

   ....

   c **What is the ratio of the phenotypes?** (1 mark, ★★)

   ....

3. **This pedigree chart shows the inheritance of colour blindness; circles represent females and squares represent males. Colour blindness is caused by a recessive sex-linked allele.**

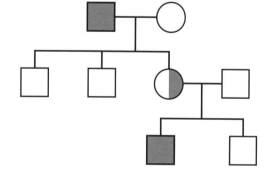

Explain why the daughter of the man with colour blindness is a carrier for colour blindness, but the sons are not. (2 marks, ★★★)

....

....

....

....

....

....

Inherited disorders

① **Cystic fibrosis is a disorder that affects the cell membranes of the lungs and pancreas. It is caused by having two copies of a recessive allele.**

a **Two parents both have one recessive allele for cystic fibrosis. Draw a Punnett square to show the genotypes of their children.** (2 marks, ★★★)

b **What is the probability that one of the children will have cystic fibrosis?** (1 mark, ★★★★)

....

 NAILIT!

Remember: probability is represented as a number between 0 and 1, not as a percentage. You can also show probability as a fraction.

NAILIT!

You need to be able to draw a Punnett square accurately and interpret the results as a ratio.

You should also be able to make predictions about the results of a genetic cross.

c **People who know that they are a carrier for cystic fibrosis may have genetic counselling. What does this mean?** (2 marks, ★★)

....

....

....

....

② **Use the example of blood groups to explain the following terms:**

a **Multiple alleles** (2 marks, ★★)

....

....

b **Codominance** (2 marks, ★★★)

....

....

Variation

1. **What are the two types of variation?** (2 marks, ★)

....

....

2. a **What is a mutation?** (2 marks, ★★)

....

....

b **Explain how mutations give rise to new variations.** (3 marks, ★★★)

....

....

....

....

c **Explain the role of new variations in natural selection.** (3 marks, ★★★★)

....

....

....

....

DO IT!

Look back at the beginning of this topic. Which type of reproduction leads to genetic mixing and therefore genetic variation in the offspring?

NAIL IT!

Explain how advantageous and disadvantageous changes in the phenotype spread or do not spread through a population.

3. **What is the Human Genome Project and why is it important?** (3 marks, ★★★)

....

....

....

Evolution

① **Put the process of natural selection into the correct order.** (4 marks, ★)

A   These individuals are more likely to have offspring.

B   Some individuals have characteristics that are better suited to the environment.

C   Individuals in a population have variation.

D   The offspring will have characteristics that are better suited to the environment.

E   These individuals are more likely to survive.

....B....   ....

② **What is evolution?** (2 marks, ★★)

....

....

....

....

③ a **Half of a population of snails living on a rocky island have brown shells and half have yellow shells. The rocks on the island are brown. New predators come to the island and begin to prey on the snails. Describe how the number of snails with each colour shell could change due to natural selection.** (4 marks, ★★★)

....

....

....

....

....

b **A scientist studying the snails wants to know if they are from the same species as the snails on a nearby island. How can they work this out?** (2 marks, ★★)

....

....

....

....

Selective breeding

(1) **Which of the following statements are true? Tick one box.** (1 mark, ★★)

A Selective breeding selects males and females with desired characteristics and breeds them together.

B In selective breeding, all of the offspring will have the desired characteristics.

C Selective breeding takes a small number of generations.

D Selective breeding is also called artificial selection.

i	A and B only	
ii	A and D only	
iii	C and D only	
iv	B and C only	

(2) **a** **A cat breeder wanted to create a breed of cats that did not cause allergies. Explain how this could be done.** (4 marks, ★★★)

....

....

....

....

b **Suggest two other reasons that people might selectively breed cats.** (2 marks, ★★)

i ....

ii ....

c **Why is it important not to breed cats that are closely related to each other?** (2 marks, ★★)

....

....

NAILIT!

Include the occurrence of recessive alleles and the consequences of inbreeding.

Genetic engineering and cloning

(1) a **What is genetic engineering?** (2 marks, ★★)

....

b **Give an example of genetic engineering.** (1 mark, ★)

....

(2) **Golden Rice is a type of rice that has been genetically engineered to contain the genes that control beta carotene production.**

a **Suggest why genetic engineering was used instead of selective breeding.** (2 marks, ★★★)

....

....

b **Give one advantage and one disadvantage of producing Golden Rice.** (2 marks, ★★)

....

....

(3) **Gene therapy has been used to treat cystic fibrosis by inserting a functional allele into cells to replace a faulty allele. Suggest why this process is not always successful.** (2 marks, ★★★)

....

....

(4) **Match the type of cloning to its method.** (3 marks, ★★)

Cuttings	Plant cells grown on sterile agar plates
Tissue culture	Splitting embryos into several smaller embryos
Embryo transplants	Section of a plant, placed into soil

(5) a **Dolly the sheep was the first animal to be cloned using adult cell cloning. Describe the process of adult cell cloning.** (5 marks, ★★★)

....

....

....

....

NAILIT!

Check what you need to know in this subtopic.

b **Evaluate the benefits and risks of adult cell cloning.** (4 marks, ★★★★)

....

....

....

Evolution and speciation

1. **Which of the following statements was an observation made by Darwin?** (1 mark, ★)

   A   Individual organisms within a particular species show a small range of variation for a characteristic.

   B   Individuals with characteristics most suited to the environment are more likely to survive and to breed successfully.

   C   The characteristics that have enabled these individuals to survive are then passed on to the next generation.

i	A and B only	
ii	B and C only	
iii	A and C only	
iv	All of the above	

   NAILIT!

   You will need to remember specific examples for the evidence of evolution.

2. **Fill in the missing words.** (4 marks, ★)

   Charles Darwin published his theory of evolution by .... in 1859. On his

   travels, he observed and collected many animal specimens and ....

   Back home, he discussed his findings with other scientists and conducted experiments on

   .... using pigeons. It was after this that he proposed his theory in his

   book, *On the Origin of* ....

3. **A population of finches was blown onto two different islands. One island had fruit trees growing on it. The other island had nut trees growing on it. After many years it was noticed that the finches on each island had different-shaped beaks.**

   a   **What type of separation is this?** (1 mark, ★)

   ....

   b   **What is the process by which the finches' beaks changed?** (1 mark, ★)

   ....

   c   **Over time, the finches were found to be separate species. Explain why they became separate species.** (4 marks, ★★★★)

   ....

   ....

   ....

   ....

The understanding of genetics

(1) The colour of peas is determined by a single gene with two alleles, one for yellow colour and the other for green colour. The yellow colour (Y) is dominant to the green colour (y).

a **What is meant by a dominant allele?** (1 mark, ★★)

....

b **If a pea plant has yellow peas, what are the possible genotypes of the plant?**
(2 marks, ★★)

....

....

c **A pea plant with yellow peas was bred with a pea plant with green peas. All of the offspring produced yellow peas. What was the genotype of the yellow pea plant?**
(2 marks, ★★★★)

Genotype ....

NAIL IT!

Draw a Punnett square to work out the answer.

(2) A plant has a tall and a short phenotype. The allele for tall plants is dominant to the allele for short plants. The tall plants have the genotype TT or Tt. The short plants have the genotype, tt.

a **A tall plant is homozygous dominant. What is its genotype?** (1 mark, ★★)

....

b **How could you describe the genotype of the short plants?** (1 mark, ★★★)

....

c **How would you describe the genotype of a tall plant that has one of each allele?**
(1 mark, ★★)

....

Classification

(1) **Complete the table below.** (4 marks, ★★)

Group	Example
Kingdom	Animal
	Vertebrate
Class	
Order	Carnivore
Family	Felidae
	Panthera
	tigris

(2) **What features are used to group organisms into different classifications of species?**
(3 marks, ★★★)

....

....

....

(3) **Carl Linnaeus proposed a system for naming organisms in the 18th century.**

   a **What did he call his system of naming organisms?** (1 mark, ★)

....

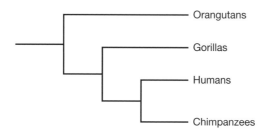

NAILIT!

You may be asked to interpret an evolutionary tree diagram like this which shows how organisms are related.

   b **Using the evolutionary tree above, explain which two species are the most closely related?** (2 marks, ★★★★)

....

....

Ecology

1 **Match the communities keywords with their meaning.** (4 marks, ★)

Keyword	Meaning
Population	The environment in which a species normally lives.
Habitat	A group of populations living and interacting with each other in the same area.
Community	A community and its abiotic environment.
Ecosystem	A group of organisms of the same species living in the same area at the same time.

2 **Organisms of different species compete with each other for resources.**

   a **Give two examples of resources that species compete for.** (2 marks, ★)

     i ....

     ii ....

   b **What is this type of competition called?** (1 mark, ★)

    ....

3 **a** **What is interdependence?** (3 marks, ★★)

    ....

    ....

    ....

   b **Ladybirds eat aphids in an apple tree. The apple tree begins to wither and several branches die. Describe and explain what will happen to the number of ladybirds and aphids.** (2 marks, ★★★)

    ....

    ....

    ....

Abiotic and biotic factors

(1) **Which of the following are biotic factors? Tick one box.** (1 mark, ★)

A Temperature

B Competition between species

C Light intensity

D Predators

i	A and C only
ii	B and D only
iii	A and B only
iv	C and D only

(2) **A researcher measured the number of sea campion plants growing on a coastal cliff edge, and the number growing 10 m inland. The results are shown in the table below.**

	Number of sea campion plants			Mean number of sea campion plants
	1	2	3	
On cliff edge	8	12	10	
10 m inland	21	22	20	

a **Complete the table above by calculating the mean number of sea campion plants in each location.** (2 marks, ★★)

b **Suggest why there are more sea campion plants 10 m inland than on the cliff edge.** (2 marks, ★★)

....

....

DO IT!

Make sure you understand and can define the following key terms:

Interdependence

....

....

Ecosystem

....

....

NAILIT!

Think about how factors such as water levels and pH of the soil allow organisms to live.

NAILIT!

You need to be able to read and interpret information from charts, graphs and tables for this topic.

3 DDT is a pesticide that is used to control the number of insects in an ecosystem. The graph below shows the amount of DDT found in different birds in the ecosystem.

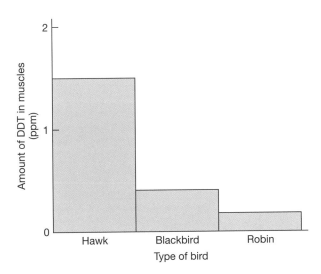

a Explain why these birds have DDT in their bodies. (1 mark, ★)

....

b Suggest why hawks have a much larger amount of DDT in their bodies than blackbirds and robins. (2 marks, ★★)

....

....

4 The graph below shows the population sizes of snowshoe hares and lynx in different years. Describe and explain the pattern of the graph. (4 marks, ★★★★)

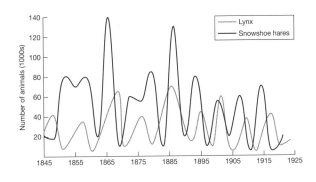

....

....

....

....

....

....

Adaptations

(1) **Adaptations enable species to survive in the condition in which they normally live. What are the different types of adaptation?** (6 marks, ★★★★)

....

....

....

....

....

....

(2) **The photo below shows a cactus plant.**

NAILIT!

Give the name of the type of adaption and include a description for each.

Describe and explain two adaptations visible in the photo which allow the cactus to live in a desert. (4 marks, ★★★)

....

....

....

....

DOIT!

Name the type of organism that lives in extreme environments.

Food chains

1 **The diagram below shows a food chain.**

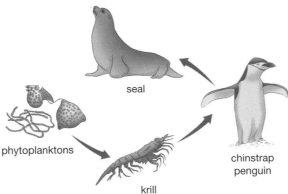

phytoplanktons

seal

krill

chinstrap penguin

a **Which organism is the producer?** (1 mark, ★)

....

b **Which organism is the tertiary consumer?** (1 mark, ★)

....

c **Where do the phytoplankton get their energy from?** (2 marks, ★)

....

....

d **Explain what would happen to the other organisms in the food chain if the numbers of krill decreased.** (3 marks, ★★★)

....

....

....

DO IT!

Mark the student's answer below using the mark scheme, and suggest how to improve the answer.

Explain why there are usually only a maximum of five or six trophic levels in a food chain. (3 marks, ★★★)

Energy is lost from each stage of the food chain. There is not enough energy at the top of the food chain.

MARK SCHEME
Energy is lost from every trophic level (1) as heat from respiration. (1) There is not enough energy at the top of the food chain for another trophic level. (1)

Number of marks for student's answer: ....

How to improve the answer: ....

....

Measuring species

(1) **A group of students were estimating the number of buttercups in a 50 m by 20 m field. They used 1 m by 1 m quadrats.**

a **What is the best method of using the quadrats?** (1 mark, ★)

  A Put several quadrats down where there are a lot of buttercups.

  B Put several quadrats down randomly on the field.

  C Place the quadrats in a line from one end of the field to the other.

  Method = ...

b **Explain why you have chosen this method.** (2 marks, ★★★)

  ....

  ....

c **The students used 10 quadrats. The number of buttercups in each quadrat are shown in the table below.**

Quadrat number	1	2	3	4	5	6	7	8	9	10	Mean
Number of buttercups	3	4	0	1	2	4	1	1	3	5	

  i **Calculate the mean number of buttercups and add it to the table.** (1 mark, ★★)

  ii **Use the mean to estimate the number of buttercups in the whole field.** (3 marks, ★★★)

  ....

  ....

  ....

NAILIT!

To estimate the number of buttercups, multiply the area of the field by the mean number of buttercups.

Investigating the relationship between organisms and their environment

(1) **A group of researchers wanted to estimate the population of snails in a woodland area.**

a **Describe and explain a good method of capturing the snails.** (2 marks, ★★)

....

....

b **The number of snails can be estimated using the 'capture, release, recapture' method. Suggest a good way of marking the snails.** (1 mark, ★)

....

c **Explain why the method of marking should not harm the snails in any way.** (2 marks, ★★)

....

....

d **The number of snails caught the first time was 10. The number of snails caught the second time was 16, and two of them were marked. Estimate the number of snails in the population.** (2 marks, ★★★)

....

....

NAILIT!

To estimate the number of snails, multiply the number of snails caught each time and divide by the number that were marked.

e **What assumptions about the population must be made in order to estimate the size of the population?** (3 marks, ★★★)

....

....

....

The carbon cycle, nitrogen cycle and water cycle

(1) **Describe how water moves through the water cycle.** (4 marks, ★★)

....

....

....

....

(2) a **What is the process by which carbon dioxide is absorbed by plants?** (1 mark, ★)

....

b **Name two processes that release carbon dioxide into the atmosphere.** (2 marks, ★)

....

....

c **Describe how the carbon in dead and decaying organisms is released back into the atmosphere.** (2 marks, ★★)

....

....

(3) **Explain why the amount of carbon dioxide in the atmosphere is greater now than it was 200 years ago.** (4 marks, ★★★)

> **NAILIT!**
>
> Think about human activities that increase the amount or prevent the uptake of carbon dioxide from the atmosphere.

....

....

....

....

(4) **A farmer wanted to add more nitrogen to the soil in a field.**

a **Describe two ways in which the farmer could do this.** (2 marks, ★★★)

....

....

b **Explain how the nitrogen is lost from the field.** (3 marks, ★★★★)

....

....

....

Decomposition

(1) Match the abiotic factors with how they influence the rate of decomposition. (3 marks, ★★)

Abiotic factor

Influence on the rate of decomposition

High temperature

Slows down or prevents the rate of decay.

Lack of water

Needed for aerobic respiration, slows down the rate of decay.

Lack of oxygen

Denatures enzymes and proteins and prevents decay.

Slows down the rate of reaction of enzymes.

(2) Gardeners and farmers often increase the rate of decay of waste biological material. Describe how they could do this. (3 marks, ★★★)

....

....

....

(3) Explain how biogas generators could be used as an alternative to fossil fuels. (3 marks, ★★★)

....

....

....

(4) A local council wishes to decrease the time it takes for them to make compost from the garden waste that they collect. Suggest how this could be done. (2 marks, ★★)

....

....

DO IT!

How do decomposers actually work? Fill in the blanks below.

Decomposers break down dead plant and animal matter by secreting _____ into the environment. Small

_____ can then _____into the microorganisms.

Investigating the effect of temperature on the rate of decay

① **A group of students were measuring the effect of temperature on the rate of decay in milk. They came up with the following method.**

- Measure 5 cm³ of milk into a boiling tube using a measuring cylinder.
- Add a drop of phenolphthalein to the milk.
- Place the milk in a 20°C water bath and time how long it takes for the phenolphthalein to change colour, using a stop clock.
- Repeat the investigation at 40°C, 60°C, 80°C and 100°C.

a **What is the independent variable in this investigation?** (1 mark, ★★)

....

b **What is the dependent variable in this investigation?** (1 mark, ★★)

....

c **What does the phenolphthalein indicator show?** (1 mark, ★)

....

d **Name one way in which you could make this investigation more reliable.** (1 mark, ★)

....

② **The results of their investigation are shown below:**

Temperature (°C)	Time taken for pH to change (s)			Mean time taken for pH to change (s)	Rate of reaction
	1	2	3		
20	230	218	242	230	0.004
40	121	132	110	121	0.008
60	260	232	256	249	0.004
80	410	421	397	409	0.002
100	530	501	522	518	0.002

a **Plot the temperature against the rate of reaction on a piece of graph paper.** (4 marks, ★★)

b **Use data from your graph to explain why milk producers heat the milk to 72°C and let it cool before selling it in the shops.** (4 marks, ★★★)

....

....

....

....

Impact of environmental change

(1) **Global warming increases the average temperature worldwide. Describe how this can affect the plants around the world.** (2 marks, ★★)

....

....

(2) a **Explain how human activity has brought about the increase in global temperatures.**
(4 marks, ★★★)

....

....

....

....

....

....

....

NAILIT!

Include the terms **deforestation** and **fossil fuels** in your answer.

b **Suggest what effect the increase in global temperatures may have on animal migration.**
(3 marks, ★★★)

....

....

....

....

....

....

STRETCHIT!

Palm oil is widely used in food and cleaning products. Find out about the environmental implications of the huge increase in palm oil farms across the globe.

Biodiversity

(1) What is biodiversity? (1 mark, ★★)

....

(2) Pollution affects biodiversity in several different ways. Match the types of pollution to their source. (3 marks, ★)

Type of pollution	Source of the pollution
Land pollution	Smoke, acidic gases from vehicle exhausts or power stations.
Air pollution	Decomposition of rubbish and from chemicals.
Water pollution	Sewage, fertiliser leeching off the fields, chemicals.

(3) Describe and explain how human activity leads to decreased biodiversity. (5 marks, ★★★★)

....

....

....

....

....

....

....

....

....

NAILIT!

All human activities affect biodiversity (whether in a positive or negative way). You need to know how land use, waste management, global warming and our use of resources affects biodiversity.

(4) Suggest how biodiversity can be increased. (3 marks, ★★★)

....

....

....

Global warming

(1) **What is global warming?** (2 marks, ★★)

....

....

(2) **Describe how greenhouses gases in the atmosphere cause global warming.** (3 marks, ★★★)

....

....

....

(3) **Describe and explain the biological consequences of global warming.** (5 marks, ★★★★)

....

....

....

....

....

....

....

....

NAILIT!

Think about how climate change and rising sea levels will affect animals.

STRETCHIT!

Global environmental policies can help to reduce the human impact on the environment. For example, the hole in the ozone layer is getting smaller because CFC gases have been banned since 1996.

What environmental policies could reduce the effect of global warming? Find out about the Paris Climate Agreement. Which aspects of this agreement relate to global warming?

Maintaining biodiversity

(1) **Name two positive human interactions that impact biodiversity.** (2 marks, ★★)

....

....

NAILIT!

Include protecting the habitat as well as protecting the animals.

(2) **Conservation areas are one way of reducing the negative effects of humans on ecosystems. Explain how they increase the biodiversity of the area.** (4 marks, ★★★★)

....

....

....

....

....

(3) **Describe and explain how breeding programs can be used to increase the biodiversity of an ecosystem.** (3 marks, ★★★)

....

....

....

DOIT!

Mark the student's answer below using the mark scheme, and suggest how to improve the answer.

Evaluate the benefits and drawbacks of a zoo-based breeding program for endangered animals.
(4 marks, ★★★)

The animals are protected from poachers and have access to medicines. However, they live in a restricted area.

MARK SCHEME

Benefits: Animals are protected from poachers (1); have medical care/vets (1).

Drawbacks: Animals live in a restricted habitat (1); decrease in genetic variation of captive population (1).

Number of marks for student's answer: ....

How to improve the answer: ....

Trophic levels and pyramids of biomass

(1) **Match the trophic levels with their descriptions.** (4 marks, ★)

Trophic level	Description
Producer	Herbivores that consume the producers.
Primary consumer	Carnivores that eat other carnivores.
Secondary consumer	Carries out photosynthesis.
Tertiary consumer	Carnivores that eat primary consumers.

(2) **A food chain is shown below.**

Phytoplankton $\longrightarrow$ Shrimp $\longrightarrow$ Penguins $\longrightarrow$ Sea lion
100 kg 70 kg 50 kg 30 kg

a **Which is the secondary consumer?** (1 mark, ★)

....

b **Which is the herbivore?** (1 mark, ★)

....

c **What does the arrow in the food chain mean?** (1 mark, ★★)

....

d **Draw the food chain as a pyramid of biomass.** (2 marks, ★★★)

NAILIT!

Don't forget to draw your pyramid of biomass to scale, e.g. 1 cm = 1 kg

e **Explain why the top of the pyramid of biomass is smaller than the bottom of the pyramid.** (2 marks, ★★)

....

....

Food production and biotechnology

(1) **What is meant by food security?** (1 mark, ★★)

....

(2) **Name two ways in which crop production can be increased.** (2 marks, ★★)

i .... ii ....

(3) **Describe how fungi can be used to make food.** (3 marks, ★★★)

....

....

....

> **NAILIT!**
>
> Genetically modified crops include crops that are drought-resistant, pesticide-resistant, and herbicide-resistant.

(4) **Biotechnology can be used to make genetically modified crops. Evaluate the advantages and disadvantages of using this technique.** (4 marks, ★★★★)

....

....

....

....

(5) **Is the statement below true or false? Justify your answer.** (3 marks, ★★★★)

> "If people reduced their intake of meat, there would be plenty of food for everyone in the world."

....

....

....

....

....

1.1 **The image below shows a plant cell.**

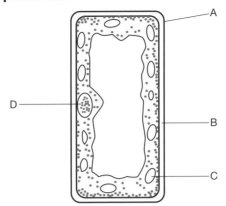

a **Label the parts of the cell A–D.** (4 marks)

A ....

B ....

C ....

D ....

b **What is the function of structure C?** (2 marks)

....

c **The ribosomes are not shown on the image. What type of microscope is needed to see small structures such as ribosomes?** (1 mark)

....

d **What is the maximum magnification and resolution of the microscope described in (c)?**
(2 marks)

Magnification ....

Resolution ....

e **The cell is actually 10 μm in diameter, but in the image it is shown at 25 mm in diameter. Calculate the magnification.** (2 marks)

Magnification = ...

1.2 a **The cell on the previous page is a specialised plant cell. How did the cell become specialised? Tick one box.** (1 mark)

Mitosis	
Differentiation	
Meiosis	
Transpiration	

b **Describe two ways in which the plant cell is different to an animal cell.** (2 marks)

....

....

1.3 a **Draw the cell cycle and label each stage.** (2 marks)

b **Describe what is happening at each stage of your cell cycle diagram.** (4 marks)

....

....

....

....

....

1.4 a **An investigation was carried out to see the effect of a drug called paclitaxel on mitosis. One onion root tip was treated with paclitaxel and another was not. After four hours, the number of cells in mitosis in each root tip was counted. The investigation was repeated three times. The results are shown in the table below.**

	Number of cells in mitosis			Mean number of cells in mitosis
	1	2	3	
Root tip treated with paclitaxel	3	4	2	
Root tip without paclitaxel	44	51	46	

i **What was the dependent variable in this investigation?** (1 mark)

....

ii **What was the independent variable in this investigation?** (1 mark)

....

b **Calculate the mean value for each row and complete the table.** (2 marks)

....

c i **Describe the results of the investigation.** (2 marks)

....

....

ii **Suggest a reason for these results.** (1 mark)

....

iii **Why was the investigation carried out three times? Tick one box.** (1 mark)

To make the results more valid	
To make the results more reliable	
To make the results more accurate	

iv **Suggest how this experiment could be improved.** (2 marks)

....

....

2.1 **Potatoes contain a lot of starch. A slice of potato is placed in a concentrated salt solution for 4 hours.**

a **The mass of the potato decreased from 5.0 g to 4.4 g. Calculate the percentage change in mass.** (2 marks)

.... %

b **Explain why the mass of the potato decreased.** (2 marks)

....

....

c Describe on a cellular level the effect of osmosis on the potato cells in the concentrated salt solution. (2 marks)

....

....

d Which food test could be used to test if the potato contained starch? (1 mark)

....

2.2 a The table below shows the results of the food tests being carried out on several unknown solutions.

Unknown solution	Sugar test	Starch test	Protein test
A	Blue	Orange	Blue
B	Blue	Blue-black	Blue
C	Green	Orange	Lilac
D	Green	Orange	Blue

i Which unknown solution could have been milk? (1 mark) ....

ii Explain your answer to (i). (2 marks)

....

....

b How is starch used in plant cells? (1 mark)

....

c A student suggests that A is sucrose. Could they be right? (1 mark)

....

d What further test could you do to test if solution A is sucrose? (2 marks)

....

....

e What type of enzyme breaks down starch in the human digestive system? Tick one box. (1 mark)

Lipase	
Protease	
Carbohydrase	

f   **Write a word equation to show how starch is broken down into smaller molecules.**
(2 marks)

....

2.3   **The image below shows a human heart.**

a   **What blood vessel is labelled A? Tick one box.** (1 mark)

Pulmonary artery	
Aorta	
Pulmonary vein	

b   **Where does A take the blood to?** (1 mark)

....

c   **Why does the blood go through the heart twice?** (2 marks)

....

....

d   **What is that type of circulation called?** (1 mark)

....

e   **Draw onto the image where the heart's pacemaker can be found.** (1 mark)

f   **Explain why it is important that the ventricles of the heart contract a short time after the atria contract.** (2 marks)

....

....

2.4 a The coronary arteries supply the heart with oxygen. Explain what will happen to the heart if the coronary arteries become blocked. (2 marks)

....

....

b How could this type of artery blockage be treated? (1 mark)

....

c Suggest **two** risk factors for coronary heart disease. (2 marks)

....

....

3.1 a Tuberculosis is caused by a bacterium. Give **three** differences between a bacterium and a eukaryotic cell. (3 marks)

....

....

....

b What type of drugs are used to treat tuberculosis? (1 mark)

....

3.2 Vaccination programs are being used worldwide to get rid of tuberculosis. The graph below shows the number of cases from tuberculosis in Madagascar between 1990 and 2015.

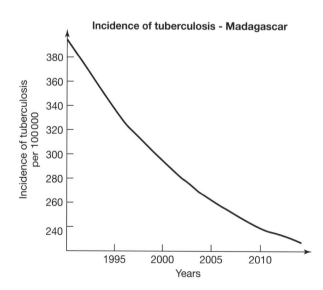

Incidence of tuberculosis - Madagascar

a **Which of the following statements is true? Tick one box.** (1 mark)

Fewer people died from tuberculosis in 2015, compared to 2010.	
In 1995, 340 people caught tuberculosis.	
There were fewer incidences of tuberculosis in 2015 compared to 2010.	

b **Describe how vaccination works.** (3 marks)

....

....

....

c **Suggest why tuberculosis is still prevalent in Madagascar.** (3 marks)

....

....

....

d **Explain what would happen to the immunity of the population if 90% or more people were vaccinated against tuberculosis.** (3 marks)

....

....

....

3.3 **Painkillers are a type of drug that inhibits pain.**

a **Give one example of a painkiller.** (1 mark)

....

b **New drugs are being discovered all the time. Name two sources of new drugs.**
(2 marks)

....

....

c A new painkiller is discovered and the scientist wants to be able to give it to the general public. What testing does the new drug have to go through first? (6 marks)

....

....

....

....

....

....

4.1 Some students are investigating the effect of light intensity on the rate of photosynthesis in pondweed. They placed a lamp at different distances from the pondweed. The students placed the pondweed underneath a glass funnel under water and measured the volume of oxygen given off using a measuring cylinder. The results are shown in the table.

Distance of lamp from pondweed	Volume of oxygen collected in 5 minutes (cm^3)	Rate of reaction (cm^3 min^{-1})
0	15.0	3.0
20	12.5	
40	6.5	
60	6	
80	6.0	

a Calculate the rates of reaction in the table. (4 marks)

b Correct any mistakes in the table. (2 marks)

....

....

c What is the independent variable in this investigation? (1 mark)

....

d **What is the dependent variable in this investigation?** (1 mark)

....

e **Name two variables that must be kept controlled throughout the investigation.** (2 marks)

....

....

f **How could the students make their data more reliable?** (1 mark)

....

4.2 a **Draw the expected shape of a graph when the rate of reaction of photosynthesis is plotted against increasing carbon dioxide levels.** (2 marks)

b **Explain the shape of the graph.** (2 marks)

....

....

c **Draw another line on the graph to show how the shape of the graph would change if the light intensity was increased.** (2 marks)

....

....

d **Explain why you have drawn the graph in this way.** (2 marks)

....

....

For an additional practice paper and the mark schemes for these, visit: www.scholastic.co.uk/gcse

Answers

For answers to the Practice Papers, visit:
www.scholastic.co.uk/gcse

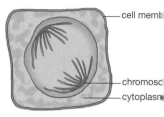

Cell biology

Eukaryotes and prokaryotes

1　a　Nucleus – B; Cytoplasm – C.

　　b　Any *two* from: This cell has a nucleus, or prokaryotic cells do not have a nucleus; This cell has does not have a cell wall, or prokaryotic cells have a cell wall; This cell does not contain plasmids, or prokaryotic cells can contain plasmids; 'Prokaryotes can have flagella' is allowed.

　　c　$0.1 \times 1000 = 100$ μm

　　d　0.6 mm

Animal and plant cells

1　Absorbs sunlight for photosynthesis – Chloroplasts; Provides strength to the cell – Cellulose cell wall; Filled with cell sap to keep the plant turgid – Permanent vacuole.

2　a　A – cellulose cell wall; B – chloroplast; C – nucleus.

　　b　Cells near the top of a leaf have more chloroplasts to absorb more sunlight; for photosynthesis.

Cell specialisation and differentiation

1　a　Many mitochondria

　　b　Any *two* from: Xylem cells; Phloem cells; Muscle cells.

　　c　To move mucus; out of the lungs OR To move an ovum; along the fallopian tube/oviduct.

2　a　A cell that is undifferentiated and can become any type of cell.

　　b　Embryo

　　c　Take stem cells and grow them in a laboratory; Expose cells to chemicals/hormones to make them differentiate into a type of specialised cell; Grow the specialised cells on a Petri dish so that they form tissues; Use the tissues to form the new organ.

Microscopy

1　a　The cells are not plant cells; There are no visible cellulose cell walls, permanent vacuole or chloroplasts.

　　b　Magnification $= \dfrac{5\,cm}{0.5\,\mu m} = \dfrac{50\,000\,\mu m}{0.5\,\mu m}$
　　　　　$= \times 100\,000$

2　Higher magnification/resolution; Able to see sub-cellular structures clearly/in detail.

3　Size of image = magnification × size of real object;
　　　　　$= 200 \times 10$;
　　　　　$= 2000$ μm or 2 mm.

Culturing microorganisms

1　a　Binary fission

　　b　Sterilise an agar plate; Spread bacteria over the surface of an agar plate using a sterile inoculating loop; Tape down the lid of the Petri dish and store the Petri dish upside down; Grow the bacteria at 25°C.

　　c　Cross-sectional area $= 3.142 \times 2.5^2$
　　　　　$= 3.142 \times 6.25$
　　　　　$= 19.64$ mm^2

　　d　Number of divisions $= 24$
　　　Number of bacteria $= 10 \times 2^{24}$
　　　　　$= 167\,772\,160$
　　　　　or 1.7×10^8

Using a light microscope

1　a　Move the lowest magnification objective lens over the specimen; Move the stage by moving the course focus, until the cells are in focus; Move the objective lens to a higher magnification, and focus using the fine focus.

　　b　To see the cells/tissues more clearly; different stains can be used to identify tissues/organelles.

　　c　×400

2　a

	Number of cells after 12 hours			
	1	2	3	Mean
With mitotic inhibitor	12	10	**11**	11
Without mitotic inhibitor	108	110	106	**108**

　　b　Any *two* from: Type of cells; Starting number of cells; Temperature; Volume of nutrient broth/culture medium.

　　c　Use different concentrations of mitotic inhibitor.

Investigating the effect of antiseptics or antibiotics

1　a　B

　　b　To prevent unwanted microorganisms from growing on the agar plate.

　　c　The clear area shows that no bacteria are growing there; Antiseptic D is inhibiting the growth of the bacteria.

　　d　Cross-sectional area $= 3.142 \times 4^2$
　　　　　$= 3.142 \times 16$
　　　　　$= 50.27$ mm^2

Mitosis and the cell cycle

1　a　G2 phase – Chromosomes are checked; S phase – Chromosomes are replicated; M phase – The cell divides into two daughter cells; Cytokinesis – Physical process of cell division.

　　b　So that when the cell divides durir mitosis; each daughter cell has the correct number of sub-cellular structures.

2　i

（cell memb）
（chromoso）
（cytoplasm）

　　ii　The replicated chromosomes are separating; to the opposite sides o the cell.

3　26 (lb)

Stem cells

1　B

2　Any *two* from: Replacing/repair of cells; Growth; Used in medical research/ treatments; Meristem used in plant clor

3　Meristem tissue; found in the shoots, roots and flowering parts of the plant.

4　Stem cells can be used to make organ for transplants, so there is no waiting time for organ donors; However, there an ethical objection to using embryos, they could potentially grow into humar animals; Using stem cells in medical treatments means that the body will not reject the cells; but there is a risk c transfer of viral infection from putting s cells into the body.

Diffusion

1　a　Diffusion is the spreading out of th particles of any substance in soluti or particles of a gas; resulting in a net movement from an area of high concentration to an area of lower concentration.

　　b　Any *one* from: In the lungs for exchange of oxygen/carbon dioxid the small intestines for the moveme of the products of digestion.

2　a　$24:8 = 3:1$;
　　　$96:64 = 3:2$
　　　　　$= 1.5:1$;

　　　Organism B has the smallest surfa area to volume ratio.

　　b　They cannot get all the substances they need by diffusion alone; They need to increase the rate of diffusie by increasing the surface area/ providing a short diffusion pathway

3　Extract solution from outside the Visk tubing; at regular intervals/named tim interval; test for the presence of gluc Factors – surface area, concentration gradient and diffusion thickness.

Osmosis

1　Osmosis is the diffusion of water from a dilute solution to a concentrated olution; through a partially permeable membrane.

From inside the cell to outside the cell.

Percentage increase $=\dfrac{(14-10)}{10} \times 100\%$

$= 40\%$

■ 3% sugar solution; because the plotted line crosses the *x*-axis at 3%.

● The same volume of water left the cell as moved into the cell.

stigating the effect of a range of centrations of salt or sugar solutions e mass of plant tissue

■ In order, the percentage change is: 16.7; 0.0; –25.0; –34.1

● No units in third column; – should be (g). 4 in second column; should be given as 4.0

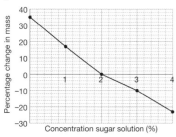

Percentage change in mass / Concentration sugar solution (%)

■ –14%

● The cells would be plasmolysed/the cell membrane would be separated from the cell wall; because water has moved from inside to outside the cell; as the water potential inside the cell is higher than the water potential outside of the cell.

·e transport

he movement of substances from a more ilute solution to a more concentrated olution; It requires energy.

he movement of mineral ions into the oot hair cells.

)smosis – Involves the movement of vater/Movement is from dilute solution to oncentrated solution; Active transport – nvolves the movement of particles/ Movement is from dilute solution to oncentrated solution.

he more mitochondria, the more espiration can be carried out; The cells the wall of the small intestine need carry out more respiration to provide nergy; for the active transport of sugars cross the wall of the small intestine.

The carrot seedlings in the aerobic conditions take up more potassium ions than the seedlings in the anaerobic conditions.

In the aerobic condition the cells can carry out aerobic respiration; and make energy for active transport to transport the potassium ions into the seedlings; In the anaerobic condition, only anaerobic respiration can be carried out which provides less energy for active transport.

Repeat the investigation to make it more reliable; Keep named variable

constant to make it more valid, e.g. temperature, surface area of seedlings, volume of water.

Tissues, organs and organ systems

The human digestive system and enzymes

1 a Any *two* from: Stomach; Small intestine; Large intestine; Pancreas; Liver; Gall bladder.

b Food mixes with saliva and travels down the oesophagus to the stomach; Food is broken down with acid and enzymes in the stomach, before moving into the small intestine; Bile from the liver, and pancreatic juices from the pancreas are added to the food in the small intestine; Digested food/named small molecules of digested food (sugars, amino acids, etc.) move from the small intestine into the bloodstream; Any food that is not digested moves into the large intestine where water is removed and a solid mass known as faeces passes out of the body through the anus.

2 a

Enzymes	Substrate	Products
carbohydrase/ amylase	carbohydrates	sugars
proteases	**proteins**	amino acids
lipases	lipids	**fatty acids and glycerol**

b Bile breaks lipids into smaller droplets/ emulsifies so that the lipase enzymes have a greater surface area to work on; Bile is alkaline and neutralises any hydrochloric acid that passes into the small intestine.

3 Food is burned inside a calorimeter; to work out the energy content in kilojoules/kJ.

4 a Proteins that can speed up chemical reactions.

b Amylase has an active site that is specific to starch; Lipids do not fit into amylase's active site.

c The rate of reaction of amylase would decrease; Amylase would denature; Starch will no longer fit in active site.

5 $24 \div 3 = 8$;

$= 8\,\text{cm}^3/\text{min}$

6

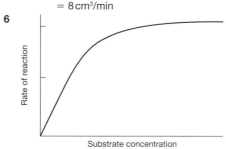

Rate of reaction / Substrate concentration

The rate of reaction of the enzyme increases as the substrate concentration increases; until all of the enzyme active sites are occupied and the rate of reaction remains constant.

Food tests

1 Starch – Iodine test; Protein – Biuret test; Lipid – Emulsion test.

2 Biuret test/Biuret reagent has been added; The sample contains/tested positive for protein.

3 Add Benedict's reagent to the sample; Heat the sample for several minutes; If the sample remains blue, there is no glucose present; If the sample turns green, yellow, orange or brick red, then glucose is present.

4 Test the solution with Benedict's reagent; if the solution turns green/yellow/orange/ brick red then maltose is present. Test the solution with biuret reagent; if the solution turns lilac then an enzyme/protein could be present.

The effect of pH on amylase

1 It is an enzyme; that breaks down starch into sugars.

2 a Amylase activity increases from pH1 to pH6; Amylase activity decreases from pH6 to pH9.

b pH6

c $10 \div 120 = 0.083\,\text{cm}^3/\text{s}$ or $5\,\text{cm}^3/\text{min}$

The heart

1 Vena cava; Pulmonary arteries; Pulmonary veins; Aorta.

2 a Blood flows from the vena cava into the right atrium which contracts; and squeezes the blood into the right ventricle; The right ventricle contracts and squeezes the blood into the pulmonary artery.

b The valves prevent the backflow of blood; between the atria and the ventricles and inside the aorta and pulmonary artery.

3 Pacemakers are a small electrical device; that can be used to regulate the contraction of the heart at rest; They can be used to correct an irregular heart rate.

The lungs

1 Air travels down the trachea; and into the bronchi; The air travels into the bronchioles; and then into the alveoli.

2 Many alveoli – Increase the surface area of the lungs; Alveolar wall is one cell thick – Gives short diffusion pathway for gases; Good supply of blood capillaries – Keeps the concentration gradient of gases high.

Blood vessels and blood

1 B and C only

2 Rate of blood flow = distance travelled by blood ÷ time

$= 2 \div 4$

$= 0.5\,\text{mm/s}$

3 Student A is correct; because arteries must have thick walls to withstand the high pressure; Arteries have narrow lumens to maintain the high pressure.

4 Any *two* from: Plasma; Platelets; Proteins; Hormones; Oxygen; Carbon dioxide.

5 A – white blood cell; B – red blood cell.

6 a Carry oxygen around the body.

b Protect the body from pathogens.

7 Phagocytes can change shape to engulf pathogens; Neutrophils have a lobed nucleus to squeeze through small spaces; Lymphocytes have a lot of rough endoplasmic reticulum to produce antibodies.

Coronary heart disease

1 A non-communicable disease that affects the heart and the coronary arteries.

2 Layers of fatty material and cholesterol build up inside the coronary arteries; and make the lumen inside the artery narrower, reducing the flow of blood to heart muscle.

3 Angina – Chest pains due to restricted blood flow to heart muscle; Heart failure – Muscle weakness in the heart muscle or a faulty valve; Heart attack – The blood supply to the heart is suddenly blocked.

4 Any *two* treatments, **with** name of treatment **and** one advantage **and** one disadvantage, from:

Stent - Advantage: holds the artery open; Disadvantage: only lasts for a few years;

Statins - Advantage: reduces blood cholesterol levels; Disadvantage: may have unwanted side effects;

Valve replacement - Advantage: heart functions properly; Disadvantage: people may object to animal valve being used;

Transplant - Advantage: heart functions properly; Disadvantage: long waiting lists for transplants/risks associated with surgery.

Health issues and effect of lifestyle

1 A disease caused by a pathogen; that can be transmitted from people or animals.

2 Any *two* from: Any viral disease; Any bacterial disease; Any fungal disease; Any protozoan disease. Check which examples your exam board requires you to know.

3 Immune system defects; make sufferers more likely to suffer infectious disease **OR** Viral infections; can be a trigger for cancer **OR** Physical ill health; could lead to mental health problems. Use specific examples if they are included for your exam board.

4 As the age of males and females increases, the number of deaths from CVD per 100 000 population increases; At each age range, the number of male deaths is greater than the number of female deaths from CVD per 100 000 population.

5 A medical condition that is not transmitted from people or animals.

6 Any *three* from: Smoking and not taking enough exercise could increase risk of cardiovascular disease; Drinking alcohol could affect liver and brain function; Smoking increases risk of lung disease and lung cancer; Smoking and alcohol could affect unborn babies.

7 Any *three* from: Person may have to change their diet; Person may have to change their level of exercise; Person may experience pain/discomfort; Person may have to pay for medicines; Person may have costs associated with hospital visits; Person may have to take time off work/be unable to work/lose income; Loss of social contact.

Cancer

1 Any *two* from: Smoking; Genetic risk factors; Drinking alcohol; Poor diet; Ionising radiation.

2 Substances in the environment/genetic factors cause mutations in DNA; that cause the cell to divide in an uncontrolled way; The cells form a mass, lying over the top of one another.

3 Benign and malignant tumours are both a growth of abnormal cells; Benign tumours are contained in one area, whereas malignant tumours can invade neighbouring tissues and spread through the blood to different parts of the body; Benign tumours do not invade other parts of the body, whereas malignant tumours form secondary tumours.

4 From 1971 to 2011, the number of cases of breast cancer in women increased; This could be because screening identified more women with breast cancer; From 1971 to 1987, the number of women dying from breast cancer remained the same, and from 1987 to 2011, the number decreased; This could be because screening identified more women as having breast cancer, and they were able to have treatment.

Plant tissues

1 Spongy mesophyll – Site of gas exchange in the leaf; Palisade tissues – The main site of photosynthesis in a leaf; Xylem – Transport of water to the leaf; Phloem – Transport of sugar sap around the plant.

2 Packed with chloroplasts to absorb light for photosynthesis; Tightly packed at the top of the leaf to absorb more light.

3

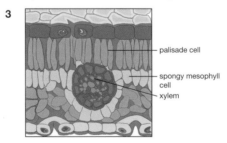

palisade cell

spongy mesophyll cell

xylem

Transpiration and translocation

1 a Potometer

b Rate of transpiration = water lost ÷ time

= 20 cm³ ÷ 5 hours

= 4 cm³/hour

2 When there is plenty of water, the cells become turgid and change shape; the pairs of guard cells no longer touch in the middle, meaning the stomata (holes) are open; Water vapour can diffuse out of the stomata; there is little water, the guard cells become flaccid and touch, closing the stomata which means water vapour can no longer diffuse out.

3 Transpiration is the loss of water from the top part of the plant; Water moves up the xylem; Translocation is the movement of sugar s around the plant; The sugar sap moves i phloem, up and down the plant.

4 Curled leaves/sunken stomata/small h to slow down the evaporation of water store water in the stems; to have avail water during the dry season.

Infection and response

Communicable (infectious) diseases

1 A microorganism that causes disease.

2 Bacterium – Tuberculosis; Fungus – Athlete's foot; Protist – Malaria.

3 In the lytic lifecycle pathway, the virus reproduces inside a host cell; then the viruses break out of the host cell; In th lysogenic lifecycle pathway, the DNA the virus is incorporated into the DNA the host cell.

4 From 1999 to 2011, the number of cas of HIV decreased from 65 to 5; This is because HIV is spread by contact with infected blood; Intravenous drug user who use the needle exchange scheme not come into contact with infected bl and are not infected with HIV.

Viral and bacterial diseases

1 Red skin rash; fever.

2 a A plant virus that affects tobacco and tomato plants; It causes a bla mosaic pattern to appear on leave

b Plants infected with TMV have a b mosaic pattern on their leaves. Th areas of the leaf cannot carry out photosynthesis.

3 Influenza is spread through coughs and sneezes; The soldiers lived close togeth so many caught influenza; When the soldiers went home, they came into con with many people; Influenza can spread direct contact with an infected person.

4 a Any *two* from: Fever; Abdominal cramps; Vomiting; Diarrhoea.

b Treated for dehydration; Antibiotic

5 a The resistant strains of bacteria are not killed by most antibiotics; mixture of antibiotics or an alterna treatment must be used.

b Any *one* from: Not practising safe sex; Not using condoms; Increase people going for testing.

Fungal and protist diseases

1 a Fungal; Black/purple spots; Photosynthesis.

b Fungicides; removing/destroying lea

2 a Any *three* from: Mosquito nets; Ins repellent; Wearing long-sleeved clothes; Taking antimalarial drugs a preventative; Using pesticides t mosquitoes.

b Mosquitoes breed in shallow pool of water; Get rid of shallow pools water to prevent breeding.

3 Destroy infected trees; Cut down heal ash trees between areas of diseased a healthy trees to prevent spread.

uman defence systems

Skin – Physical barrier against pathogens; Nose – Small hairs and mucus trap airborne particles; Trachea – Cilia move mucus up to the throat; Stomach – Hydrochloric acid and proteases kill pathogens; Tears – Contain lysozymes which kill bacteria.

a   Phagocytes; lymphocytes.

b   Lymphocytes produce antibodies; The antibodies attach to pathogens and prevent them from entering cells; The antibodies attach to pathogens and target them for phagocytosis; Macrophages engulf targeted pathogens; Antibodies act as antitoxins by attaching to toxins released by the pathogen.

ccination

Inactive; pathogen; white blood cells/lymphocytes.

Vaccines contain a dead or inactive pathogen which acts as an antigen; When this is injected into the body, it stimulates white blood cells/lymphocytes to produce antibodies; The antibodies bind specifically to the pathogen's antigens; If the vaccinated person is infected with the same pathogen, the antibodies bind to the pathogen to fight the disease.

Prevents/irradicates diseases; may have side effects.

tibiotics and painkillers

Any antibiotic, e.g. penicillin/erythromycin; Any painkiller, e.g. paracetamol/ibuprofen.

They kill bacteria that have infected the body; Some specific bacteria are killed by a specific type of antibiotic.

Antiviral drugs kill viruses while they are outside the body's cells; If a virus enters a cell, the antiviral drug cannot kill it.

Ibuprofen reduces pain more than glucosamine sulfate does; Glucosamine sulfate reduces pain for eight weeks, whereas ibuprofen reduces pain for two weeks.

Control prescriptions of antibiotics; make sure patients take the full course of antibiotics; discover new antibiotics.

v drugs

Aspirin – Willow bark; Digitalis – Foxgloves; Penicillin – *Penicillium*.

By extracting compounds from plants or microorganisms; By altering already existing compounds.

During preclinical testing new drugs are tested on cells to test for toxicity/efficacy/correct dose; If the drug is safe it goes to clinical trial, where a low dose is given to healthy volunteers to check for toxicity; Then different doses are given to healthy volunteers and patients to find the optimum dose; Finally, the drug is given to patients and compared with another drug or placebo to test how effective it is.

Monoclonal antibodies and their uses

1   Lymphocytes

2   They bind specifically to a particular antigen; The shape of the antibody is complementary to the shape of the antigen.

3   Inject a mouse with an antigen; to stimulate one of the mouse lymphocytes to form many clones of itself; These cloned lymphocytes make antibodies that are complementary in shape to the antigen; The lymphocytes are combined with a type of tumour cell to make hybridoma cells; The hybridoma cells divide and make antibodies.

4   Any *two* from: Pregnancy tests; Disease detection; Blood testing; Research; Treating diseases.

5   Any *two* from: Allergic reaction; Chills; Fever; Rashes; Feeling sick; Breathlessness.

6   Monoclonal antibodies are very specific/they will only bind to a particular antigen, so they can be used to detect molecules. Will only bind to cancer cells, so can deliver medicines without harming healthy cells; May cause discomfort to the animals that are being used to make monoclonal antibodies; Using monoclonal antibodies in treatments may have side effects.

Plant diseases and defences

1   3. Yellowing of the leaves; caused by lack of sunlight or a mineral ion deficiency.

2   Aphids are pests that cause malformed stems.

3   Use a gardening manual/website; Take the infected plant to a laboratory; Diseases can be detected in plants by looking at their growth and colour of their leaves; Pathogens can be detected using kits containing monoclonal antibodies.

4   a   Look for poor growth and yellow leaves.

    b   Nitrates are needed to make proteins; which are needed for growth and healthy leaves.

5   Any *two* from: Cellulose cell walls around plant cells; Bark on the trunk of a tree; Waxy cuticle on leaves.

6   Antibacterial chemicals; to defend plants against pathogens **OR** Poisons/toxins in the leaves; to sting any herbivores that try to eat them.

7   Thin, spiky leaves are difficult for animals to eat; The leaves will not be eaten, allowing the plant to carry out more photosynthesis; Pine cones are covered in a hard, tough material that is difficult for animals to eat; The seeds inside are protected from being eaten and can grow into new pine trees.

Bioenergetics

Photosynthesis

1   a   Carbon dioxide + water $\xrightarrow{\text{light}}$ glucose + oxygen

b   Endothermic reaction (two stage reaction is allowed for OCR students).

c   Carbon dioxide is a reactant in photosynthesis; It supplies the carbon to make glucose.

d   Any *four* from: Place an aquatic plant in a funnel under water; Measure the volume of oxygen given off in a given time; Repeat the experiment at different given temperatures; Repeat investigation at least twice; Calculate the rate of reaction at each temperature.

Rate of photosynthesis

1   Any *one* from: Increased light; increased temperature; Increased carbon dioxide concentration; Increased amount of chlorophyll.

2   a   An environmental condition; that limits the rate of photosynthesis.

    b   B

3   Rate of photosynthesis = $\dfrac{\text{oxygen given off}}{\text{time}}$

$= 24 \div 4$

$= 6\,cm^3/min$

Investigating the effect of light intensity on the rate of photosynthesis

1   a   Independent variable: distance of the lamp from the plant; Dependent variable: volume of oxygen.

    b   Make sure that the lamp is the only light source; Keep the room at the same temperature/stand tube with pond weed in a beaker of water; Use the same piece of pondweed.

    c   In order from top to bottom: 39, 17, 8, 2.

    d   Light energy is needed for photosynthesis to occur.

Uses of glucose

1   Any *two* from: Used in respiration, to release energy; Converted into starch for storage; Used to produce oil for storage; Used to produce amino acids for protein synthesis; Used to produce cellulose for cell walls.

2   Glucose has the chemical formula $C_6H_{12}O_6$.

3   By the process of photosynthesis.

Respiration and metabolism

1   a   Glucose + oxygen → carbon dioxide + water

    b   Exothermic

2   a   Mitochondria

    b $C_6H_{12}O_6 + 6O_2 \rightarrow 6CO_2 + 6H_2O$

3   Respiration happens in the absence of oxygen for a short time; Glucose is converted to lactic acid. Lactic acid builds up in the muscles, causing muscle fatigue.

4   Place the yeast into a test tube, with sodium hydroxide/potassium hydroxide to absorb carbon dioxide; measure the volume of oxygen being given off by the yeast; using a respirometer/gas syringe/capillary tube.

Answers

5 Respiration; Breakdown of excess proteins to urea for excretion in urine.

6 Energy is needed to form new bonds when making new complex molecules; Energy is needed to break bonds when breaking complex molecules into simpler ones.

Response to exercise

1 a Find pulse in wrist/radial artery or neck/carotid artery; Count the number of pulses in 15 seconds; and multiply the number by four.

   b 18 x 4 = 72 beats per minute.

2 a Any *two* statements *with* reasons: Increase in heart rate; so that blood flows to the cells more quickly; Increase in breathing rate; to oxygenate the blood more quickly/remove carbon dioxide quickly; Increase in breath volume; to take in more oxygen with each breath; Increased rate of respiration in muscle cells/increased production of energy.

   b 80 x 60; 4800 cm^3 per minute/4.8 dm^3 per minute.

3 He still needs to remove extra carbon dioxide; He will have carried out some anaerobic respiration; and lactic acid would have been made; The lactic acid needs to be broken down by oxygen.

Homeostasis and response

Homeostasis

1 Homeostasis keeps all the internal conditions of the body constant/the same, whatever the outside conditions might be.

2 a Controlling the internal temperature of the body; Controlling the water levels in the body.

   b When the blood glucose concentration is too high, insulin is released by the pancreas; Insulin causes cells to take up glucose, so the blood glucose concentration returns to normal; In the liver, excess glucose is converted to glycogen for storage;
   When the blood glucose concentration is too low, glucagon is released by the pancreas; Glycogen is broken down into glucose and more glucose is released, so the blood glucose concentration returns to normal.

3 The brain is the coordinator in homeostasis; It receives and processes information from receptors; It sends nerve impulses to effectors to restore optimum conditions.

The human nervous system and reflexes

1 C

2 a Stimulus → receptor → coordinator → effector → response (mark for each)

   b To receive nerve impulses from the receptor; and send nerve impulses to the effectors.

3 The light stimulus is detected by the receptor; A nerve impulse is sent to the coordinator; The coordinator sends nerve impulses to the effectors; The response is for the hand to press the button.

4 Any *two* from: Sensory neurones; Motor neurones; Relay neurones.

5 Sensory neurones have their cell body near the centre of the axon, but motor and relay neurones have their cell body at the end of the axon;
   Sensory neurones carry nerve impulses to the central nervous system, motor neurones carry nerve impulses from the central nervous system and relay neurones carry nerve impulses from sensory neurones to motor neurones;
   Relay neurones are only used in reflex arcs, but sensory and motor neurones are used in reflex arcs and voluntary reactions.

6 a Reflexes are automatic, but voluntary reactions are under conscious control; Reflexes are quicker than voluntary reactions.

   b Protection from harm; Voluntary reaction times are too slow.

Investigating the effect of a factor on human reaction time

1 a Repeat investigation three times; Measure out same volume of cola each time; Repeat investigation at the same time of day each time; Leave the same time interval between drinking cola and measuring reaction times.

   b

Condition	Reaction time 1 (s)	Reaction time 2 (s)	Reaction time 3 (s)	Mean reaction time (s)
Before caffeine	0.55	0.45	0.50	
After caffeine	0.40	0.35	0.30	

   c

Condition	Reaction time 1 (s)	Reaction time 2 (s)	Reaction time 3 (s)	Mean reaction time (s)
Before caffeine	0.55	0.45	0.50	0.50 (1)
After caffeine	0.40	0.35	0.30	0.35 (1)

The brain and the eye

1 A – Cerebral cortex; B – Cerebellum; C – Medulla.

2 a Balance; Coordinated movements.

   b Any *two* from: Conscious thought; Memory; Language; Learning.

3 Electrical stimulation and MRI.

4 A – Iris; B – Retina; C – Cornea; D – Lens.

5 a Controls the amount of light entering the eye.

   b Prevents too much light entering the eye in bright light; Allows more light to enter the eye in low light conditions.

Focusing the eye

1 a Accommodation is the process of changing the shape of the lens to focus on near or distant objects.

   b The ciliary muscles contract; and the suspensory ligaments loosen; The len becomes thicker and refracts light ray strongly to focus light onto the retina.

   c i Distant objects do not focus clearly; The image is focused in front of the retina.

      ii Concave lens

      iii The concave lens refracts the lig so that the image is focussed on the retina.

      iv Difficulty distinguishing between colours, especially red and green

   d Clouding of the lens; Light cannot pa into the eye.

Control of body temperature

1 Vasoconstriction/blood vessels close to the skin constrict; Shivering.

2 Any *two* from: Shivering, confusion, fatigue, rapid and shallow breathing, blu appearance and loss of consciousness.

3 Monitored by the thermoregulatory cen in the brain; Thermoreceptors in the thermoregulatory centre and in the skin monitor the temperature of the blood and skin; When these detect a change in temperature, they send electrical impulses to the thermoregulatory centre The thermoregulatory centre sends nerve impulse to effectors; to bring the body temperature back to the optimum temperature.

Human endocrine system

1 Pituitary gland—Growth hormone, FSH and LH; Pancreas—Insulin and glucago Thyroid—Thyroxine; Ovary—Progester and oestrogen.

2 The pituitary gland in the brain controls many of the other glands in the body; b releasing hormones that affect them.

3 The nervous system targets effectors more quickly than the endocrine syster The nervous system uses nerves/neurc and the endocrine system uses hormo The effects of the nervous system last a short time whereas the effects of the endocrine system last for a long time; nervous system is controlled by the bra and the endocrine system is controlled the pituitary gland.

Control of blood glucose concentration

1 Pancreas

2 Cells take up glucose; Glucose is converted into glycogen; in the liver ar muscle cells.

3 Glucagon converts glycogen into glucose; in the liver and muscle cells; This increases the concentration of blc glucose in the blood.

Any *two* from: The cells in the body would not take in glucose; The cells would have less glucose for respiration; The person would feel tired.

ᵇetes

Disease where no insulin is produced; or the body stops responding to insulin.

When the blood sugar level is too high.

In type 1 diabetes, the body does not release insulin, but in type 2 diabetes the body stops responding to insulin; Type 1 diabetes has a genetic cause, but type 2 diabetes is caused by lifestyle factors; such as obesity and poor diet; Type 1 diabetes is treated by injecting insulin but type 2 diabetes is treated with a carbohydrate-controlled diet and exercise.

The blood sugar levels rise after a meal; and remain high for several hours.

ᵗaining water and nitrogen balance in ᵇody

■ The diffusion of water from a more dilute solution to a more concentrated solution.

▶ Water will move out of the cells; The cells could become shrivelled/crenated.

In the glomerulus, glucose moves out of the blood and into the Bowman's capsule; by ultrafiltration; Glucose moves into the nephron because it is a small molecule; but is selectively reabsorbed back into the blood.

Medulla; ureter; pelvis labeled in the correct place on the diagram.

A hormone; that acts on the kidneys to reduce the amount of water lost in urine.

If there is too little water, the blood is too concentrated; and the hypothalamus causes the pituitary gland to release ADH; If there is too much water, the blood is too dilute; and the hypothalamus causes the pituitary gland to stop releasing ADH.

ADH travels in the blood to the kidneys; ADH causes the collecting duct to be more permeable to water; so more water leaves the collecting duct, and moves back into the blood.

ᵃˢis

Filters the blood of people with kidney disease; and removes excess ions, excess water and urea. The blood moves through the dialysis machine, where it is separated from the dialysate; by a partially permeable membrane; The concentration of urea is higher in the blood compared to the dialysate, so this moves into the dialysate down a concentration gradient by diffusion; If the ion concentration in the blood is higher than the dialysate, the ions move into the dialysate by diffusion.

A kidney transplant would mean that there would be no need for dialysis, which is time consuming; However, there is a shortage of kidney donors/risk of rejection/need to take immunosuppressant drugs; Dialysis

is available/no need for surgery; However, dialysis is time consuming/carries a risk of infection/patients must limit protein in their diet.

3 Potassium levels need to be kept balanced, healthy kidneys excrete excess potassium in the urine. Dialysis removes excess potassium but only when it is taking place - cannot in between which is when orange juice should be avoided.

Hormones in human reproduction

1 Testosterone – Testes; Oestrogen – Ovaries; Follicle – stimulating hormone – Pituitary gland.

2 **a** Causes eggs in the ovaries to mature.

   b Oestrogen

3 **a** LH stimulates the ovaries to release an egg/ovulation.

   b Progesterone maintains the lining of the uterus; If the egg released on day 14 is fertilised, then it will implant into this lining.

Contraception

1 Condoms – Trap sperm; Intrauterine device (IUD) – Prevents implantation of an embryo; Spermicidal agents – Kill sperm.

2 **a** Any *two* from: Oral contraceptives; Hormone injection; Hormone skin patch; Hormone implant.

   b Oral contraceptives contain oestrogen and progesterone; so that FSH is inhibited, and no eggs mature; Other hormonal contraceptives contain progesterone to inhibit the maturation and release of eggs.

3 Any *four* from: Oral contraceptives/ intrauterine devices are effective at preventing pregnancy, but have some side effects on the female body; Condoms/ diaphragms/spermicidal agents do not have any side effects, but are not 100% effective at preventing pregnancy; Surgical methods are very effective at preventing pregnancy but are difficult to reverse; Condoms and oral contraceptives allow couples to choose the time to start a family; Abstaining from intercourse around the time that an egg may be in the oviducts does not have any side effects on the body, but is difficult to use to prevent pregnancy as menstruation cycles and ovulation dates can fluctuate.

Using hormones to treat infertility

1 **iii** A and C only

2 FSH and LH are given to the woman in order to produce enough eggs for IVF; Eggs are surgically removed from the woman and fertilised by the man's sperm in a laboratory; The fertilised eggs develop into embryos and then placed surgically into the woman's uterus.

3 IVF allows the mother to give birth to her own baby; The baby will be the genetic offspring of the mother and father; However, the success rates are not high; and it can lead to multiple births.

Negative feedback

1 A mechanism that keeps the body functioning at set levels; If something goes above or below the set level, negative feedback brings it back again.

2 **a** Adrenal glands.

   b **iii** A, B and D only

3 When the level of thyroxine in the blood is low, the hypothalamus releases TRH, which stimulates the anterior pituitary to release TSH, which stimulates the thyroid gland to release thyroxine; TSH inhibits the hypothalamus producing TRH; When the level of thyroxine is high, it inhibits both the hypothalamus producing TRH and the anterior pituitary producing TSH.

Plant hormones

1 Phototropism – light; Geotropism – gravity; Hydrotropism – water

2 Auxin causes the cells in the shoot to elongate; More auxin gathers on the side of the shoot that is in the shade; This makes the cells on the shaded side elongate more than the cells on the non-shaded part of the shoot; This causes the shoot tip to bend in the direction of the light.

3 In the shoot tips, there is more auxin on the side of the shoot that is facing downwards; Auxin stimulates these cells to elongate more than the cells on the side of the shoot that is facing upwards, so the shoot tip bends upwards; In the root tips, more auxin gathers on the side of the root that is facing downwards; Auxin inhibits the elongation of these cells, so they elongate less than the cells on the side of the root tip that is facing upwards, causing the root tip to bend down.

4 Gibberellins initiate seed germination; Ethene controls cell division/ripens fruits.

Investigating the effect of light or gravity on the growth of newly germinated seedlings

1 Mistake – units missing from column three; Correction – Length of shoot (cm)
   or
   Mistake – number in column three, row two to 1 s.f.; Correction – 2.0

2 Any *two* from: Same light source; Same distance from the germinated seedling; Same germinated seedling.

3 Auxin gathers on the shaded part of the shoot each time the light is moved; This causes the cells on the shaded part of the shoot to elongate; This bends the shoot towards the light.

4 Auxins – weedkiller, rooting powder, tissue culture; Gibberellins – end of seed dormancy, promotion of flowering, fruit size.

Inheritance, variation and evolution

Sexual and asexual reproduction

1 **a** Female – Egg/ovum; Male – Sperm.

   b Meiosis

2 Bacteria – Binary fission; Yeast – Budding; Strawberry plants – Runners; Potatoes – Tubers.

Answers

3 Sexual reproduction produces variation in the offspring, which gives a selective advantage in natural selection; However, you need to find two parents in order to have sexual reproduction; Asexual reproduction produces many identical offspring quickly; However, genetically identical offspring are vulnerable to changes in the environment.

Meiosis

1 Mitosis: 2, Full, Yes; Meiosis: 4, Half, No.

2 Meiosis goes through two rounds of cell division to produce four daughter cells; Each daughter cell has half of the number of chromosomes as the original body cell; The chromosomes are randomly assorted into the four daughter cells so that they are genetically different from each other.

3 A male and a female gamete join together and the two nuclei fuse; When this happens, the new cell/zygote has a full set of chromosomes; The zygote divides many times by mitosis to form an embryo.

DNA and the genome

1 iii A, B and D only

2 a 46 chromosomes

b 19 chromosomes

3 To find out which genes are linked to diseases; To learn how to treat inherited diseases; To trace human migration patterns from the past.

4 The soap is needed to break down the cell membrane and nuclear envelope/membrane; the DNA will form a precipitate in the ethanol and become visible; ice-cold ethanol will prevent enzymes in the solution digesting the DNA.

DNA structure

1 a

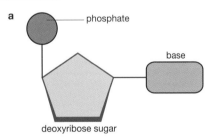

(Circle labelled phosphate/phosphate group; Attached to pentagon labelled deoxyribose sugar; Hexagon/rectangle labelled as base/nitrogenous base)

b Polynucleotide

2 A base pairs with T; C base pairs with G; The bases are held together by hydrogen bonds.

3 A sequence of three bases codes for a particular amino acid; The order of the bases controls the order in which the amino acids are added to the polypeptide; This makes a particular protein.

Protein synthesis

1 C F A E D B or C F A D E B.

2 The polypeptide chain folds into a 3D shape; depending on the sequence of amino acids.

3 a Substitution mutations could alter a three base code; which would alter the amino acid sequence of a protein; If this affects the shape of the protein, then the protein may no longer be able to function.

b The non-coding DNA controls whether the genes are switched on or off; A change in the base sequence of the non-coding DNA could change whether the gene is switched on or off.

Genetic inheritance

1 Homozygous – When two copies of the same allele are present; Heterozygous – When two different alleles are present; Genotype – The alleles that are present in the genome; Phenotype – The characteristics that are expressed by those alleles.

2 a

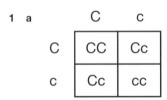

	B	b
b	Bb	bb
b	Bb	bb

b Black or brown

c 1:1

3 The allele for colour blindness is carried on the X chromosome; The daughter has inherited one X chromosome from her father, but the two sons have inherited a Y chromosome from their father.

Inherited disorders

1 a

	C	c
C	CC	Cc
c	Cc	cc

b 1/4 or 0.25

c They will discuss the chances of having a child with cystic fibrosis; They may decide not to have children/use embryo screening.

2 a When there are three or more alleles; Blood groups have the alleles, A, B and O.

b When two alleles are both expressed; Alleles A and B are both expressed in the genotype, AB.

Variation

1 Genetic; Environmental

2 a A change in the base sequence of the DNA; Can be a base change/substitution, deletion or addition of bases.

b A change in the base sequence changes the three base code that decides the sequence of amino acids; The amino acid sequence of the polypeptide changes; The shape of the protein changes.

c If the new variation has little influence on the phenotype, then there will

be no advantage to the organism; If the new variation changes the phenotype but is not advantageou to the organism, then the organism less likely to have offspring and the new variation will not spread throu the population; If the new variation changes the phenotype and it is advantageous to the organism, tho with the advantageous phenotype more likely to survive and reproduc passing the new allele to their offspring. Over many generations the numbers with the mutation will increase.

3 The sequencing of the entire human genome; used to find out which gene codes for each protein; allows researc into inheritable diseases/new drug targ for medicine.

Evolution

1 C B E A D

2 The process by which complex living organisms; gradually evolved from sim organisms by natural selection.

3 a The brown snails are less easy for predators to spot against the brow background; They are more likely t survive; and produce offspring; Ov time, more of the snail population have brown shells.

b They are the same species if they can interbreed; and produce fertile offspring.

Selective breeding

1 ii A and D only

2 a Breed together a male and a fema cat that do not cause allergies; Se any offspring that also do not cau allergies; Breed these offspring wi other cats that do not cause allerg Keep breeding until all of the offsp do not cause allergies.

b Any *two* from: Long/short fur; Temperament; Short claws; Coat/c colour; *Any sensible answer.*

c More likely to have two copies of a recessive allele; More likely to bec ill/have disorders.

Genetic engineering and cloning

1 a The addition of a gene from anoth organism; into an organism's geno

b Any from: Disease-resistant plants Plants that produce bigger fruits; Bacteria that produce human insu Gene therapy; *Any sensible answe*

2 a Rice plants do not contain the ger that control beta carotene product Selective breeding takes many generations, genetic engineering t one generation.

b Advantage - Makes the rice more nutritious/prevents vitamin A deficiency; Disadvantage - Could potentially cause harm/difficult to genes into the right place.

t is not always possible to get the
functional allele into the cells; The allele
may not be expressed by the cells.

Cuttings—Section of a plant, placed into
soil; Tissue culture—Plant cells grown on
sterile agar plates; Embryo transplants—
Splitting embryos into several smaller
embryos.

a An adult body cell is removed from
one animal, and an egg from another
animal; The nucleus is removed from
the egg; The nucleus from the body
cell is inserted into the egg; An electric
shock stimulates the egg to divide to
form an embryo; When the embryo
has developed into a ball of cells, it
is inserted into the uterus of an adult
female.

b Able to produce many organisms
with the desired characteristics; Able
to make large numbers of more rare
species; All clones will be susceptible to
the same diseases; The clones will have
no variation, and so will not be able to
respond to changes in the environment.

ution and speciation

i B and C only

Natural selection; Fossils; Selective
breeding; Species;

a Geographical separation

b Natural selection

c The two populations have different
selective pressures, due to the
different food sources; The finches
with the best-shaped beaks to eat
the food are more likely to survive;
and pass on their advantageous
characteristic to their offspring;
Eventually the two populations will
no longer be able to interbreed and
produce fertile offspring.

understanding of genetics

An allele that is always expressed in
the phenotype.

b YY; Yy

c YY

d TT

Homozygous recessive

Heterozygous

sification

Group	Example
Kingdom	Animal
Phylum	Vertebrate
Class	**Mammal**
Order	Carnivore
Family	Felidae
Genus	Panthera
Species	tigris

according to: anatomy: physiology: and
behaviour.

3 a Binomial system

b Humans and chimpanzees; because
the branches on the evolutionary tree
branched off from each other the most
recently.

Ecology

Communities

1 Population—A group of organisms of the
same species living in the same area at
the same time;

Habitat—The environment in which a
species normally lives;

Community—A group of populations living
and interacting with each other in the
same area;

Ecosystem—A community and its abiotic
environment.

2 a Any *two* from: Food; Water; Territory/
space; Light; Mineral ions.

b Interspecific competition

3 a When species depend on each
other for survival; They depend on
each other to provide food/shelter/
pollination/seed dispersal; If one
species is removed from a habitat, it
can affect the whole community.

b The number of aphids will decrease,
as their food source decreases; The
number of ladybirds will also decrease,
as their food source decreases.

Abiotic and biotic factors

1 ii B and D only

2 a 10, 21

b The cliff edge is very windy; and
removes a lot of moisture from the
soil, making it more difficult for the
sea campion plants to grow.

3 a The birds eat the insects that have
been killed by DDT.

b The hawks are further up the food
chain/top predators; DDT accumulates
in the organisms as it moves up the
food chain.

4 Just after the prey/snowshoe hare
population increases, the predator lynx
population increases; This is because
the snowshoe hares are a food source
for the lynx, and provide energy for the
lynx to reproduce; Just after the prey/
snowshoe hare population decreases, the
predator/lynx population decreases; This
is because the lynx do not have as much
food and some will die of starvation.

Adaptations

1 Structural adaptations; are adaptations
to the body of the organism; Behavioural
adaptations; are changes to a species'
behaviour to help their survival; A
functional adaptation; is one that has
occurred through natural selection over
many generations in order to overcome a
functional problem.

2 Cactus has needles; to reduce water loss/
prevent evaporation from the plant; Water
storage in the stem of the cactus; ensures
the cactus has a supply of water when
there is no rain/no water available.

Food chains

1 a Phytoplankton

b Seal

c From sunlight; through
photosynthesis.

d The amount of phytoplankton
would increase because the primary
consumers would not be eating them;
The number of chinstrap penguins
would decrease because there would
be fewer krill for them to eat; The
number of seals would decrease
because there would be fewer
chinstrap penguins for them to eat.

Measuring species

1 a B

b Removes bias; and makes sure that
the sample is representative.

c i 2.4

ii Area of the field = 50 m
= 1000 m^2

2.4 x 1000 m^2; = 2400 buttercups.

Investigating the relationship between organisms and their environment

1 a Pitfall traps; because the snails move
along the ground.

b Using a non-toxic paint/marker pen/
sticker on the shell.

c If the paint/pen is toxic it could kill the
snail; If the paint/pen/sticker is bright it
may attract predators to eat the snail.

d (10 x 16)/2 = 80 snails

e Snails had time to mingle with the rest
of the population; No snails migrated;
No snails died or were born.

The carbon cycle, nitrogen cycle and water cycle

1 Water in the oceans evaporates into the
atmosphere; The water droplets condense
to form clouds and are transported inland
by the wind; As the clouds rise, the water
droplets are released as precipitation; The
water moves into streams and rivers, and
back to the oceans.

2 a Photosynthesis

b Aerobic respiration; Combustion

c Dead and decaying organisms are
decomposed by bacteria and fungi/the
decomposers; which release carbon
dioxide through aerobic respiration.

3 The number of people has increased;
and the amount of deforestation has
increased as we make room for housing
and fields to grow food so less carbon
dioxide is removed from the atmosphere
by photosynthesis. More fossil fuels
are being burned by combustion as we
increase the use of cars/power plants.
An increase in industrial processes has
increased the amount of carbon dioxide
released into the atmosphere.

Answers

4 a Adding fertiliser/nitrates/manure; growing leguminous plants/peas/clover.

   b Plants are consumed by animals; Fertilisers leach off the fields during rainfall; Nitrates in the soil are converted into atmospheric nitrogen by bacteria in the soil.

Decomposition

1 High temperature — Denatures enzymes and proteins and prevents decay.
Lack of water — Slows down or prevents the rate of decay.
Lack of oxygen — Needed for aerobic respiration, slows down the rate of decay.

2 Using the optimum temperature/pH; Aerate the decaying matter; Introduce detritivores/worms/woodlice to break down the decaying matter into smaller pieces.

3 Microorganisms decompose the waste anaerobically to produce methane gas, which can be used as a fuel.

4 Put the waste into a tank where the optimum conditions could be tightly regulated/monitored. Make sure the garden waste was turned regularly to mix in the oxygen.

Investigating the effect of temperature on the rate of decay

1 a Temperature

   b Time for indicator to change colour/pH to change

   c When the pH of the milk has decreased (below pH8).

   d Repeat the investigation/Use a standard to compare the end point of the reaction.

2 a Temperature on x axis, rate of reaction on y axis; Axes correctly plotted; Units included on x axis; All points correctly plotted.

   b At 72°C a lot of the bacteria in milk will be killed/the proteins/enzymes in the bacteria will be denatured; It slows down the rate of decay in milk.

Impact of environmental change

1 If the temperature increases, it may reduce the amount of water available for plants; The plants could die, causing desertification.

2 a Deforestation increases the amount of land for houses and farming; However, the decrease in the number of trees decreases the amount of photosynthesis; and this increases the amount of carbon dioxide in the atmosphere; Human activity, such as burning fossil fuels, also increases the amount of carbon dioxide in the atmosphere. Carbon dioxide is a greenhouse gas so traps heat in our atmosphere; As levels of carbon dioxide increase so does the amount of heat trapped and the global temperature.

   b Species may migrate to an area where the temperature is more suitable, and there is available water; Sometimes the changes in temperature and water availability are seasonal, and species migrate between geographical areas for a season.

Biodiversity

1 The variety of living species of organisms on the Earth, or within an ecosystem.

2 Land pollution—Decomposition of landfill and from chemicals; Water pollution - Sewage, fertiliser leeching off the fields, chemicals; Air pollution - Smoke, acidic gases from vehicle exhausts or power stations.

3 As humans increase in number, there is an increase in deforestation, to provide land for houses and farming; Farming large areas with the removal of hedgerows and the planting of one crop (monoculture) decreases biodiversity; Humans use more resources which creates more pollution destroying habitats for other organisms; Humans burn fossil fuels which leads to increased carbon dioxide in the atmosphere and leads to global warming; This leads to climate change that decreases biodiversity.

4 Decrease pollution; Decrease deforestation; Decrease global warming.

Global warming

1 Increase in global temperature; caused by an increase in greenhouse gases in the atmosphere.

2 Radiation from the Sun warms the earth, and this heat is reflected from the Earth's surface; The greenhouses gases in the atmosphere absorb the heat; increasing the temperature of the atmosphere.

3 Global weather patterns will change causing flooding in some areas and drought in other areas; This will decrease available habitats, and food and water availability; Sea levels will rise; decreasing available habitats; Increased migration of organisms as species will move to more suitable habitats with enough available water and food; There will be an increased extinction of species, as some species will not be able to migrate or adapt quickly enough to the changing climate.

Maintaining biodiversity

1 Any *two* from: Conservation areas; Using renewable energy; Recycling waste; Reducing waste and pollution; Fish farming; Sustainable farming methods.

2 Protects endangered species from being hunted; Keeps species in their original habitat; Protects rare habitats; Reduces deforestation; the more habitats which are maintained, the greater the variety of food, so a wider variety of species can be supported.

3 Species can be protected in captivity; build up the numbers of the population. The species can then be released back into their natural ecosystem.

Trophic levels and pyramids of biomass

1 Producer—Carry out photosynthesis; Primary consumer - Herbivores that consume the producers; Secondary consumer - Carnivores that eat primary consumers; Tertiary consumer—Carnivores that eat other carnivores.

2 a Penguins

   b Shrimp

   c Transfer of energy

   d Pyramid should be drawn to scale. Suggest 10cm width for phytoplankton, 7cm width for shrimp, 5cm width for penguins and 3cm width for seals.

     Phytoplankton should be at the bottom, then shrimp, penguins and sea lions.

   e There is more energy at the bottom of the pyramid; The energy is gradually lost as it moves up the food chain.

Food production and biotechnology

1 Having enough food to feed a population.

2 Any *two* from: Using fertilisers; Using pesticides; Using herbicides; Using genetically modified crops; Growing crops in a greenhouse.

3 Fungus/*Fusarium* is used to make mycoprotein; grown inside a fermenter with a glucose-rich broth and mixed with oxygen.

4 Advantages – any *two* from: Drought-resistant crops can be grown in areas where there is less water; Pesticide-resistant crops are less likely to be eaten by pests so there is a higher yield; Herbicide-resistant crops will not be affected by spraying the crop with herbicides so there is a higher yield.

   Disadvantages – any *two* from: Genes may be spread to other species; Possibility that genetic modification may cause harm to consumers; People may not like the idea of consuming genetically modified crops.

5 True; because farming animals takes up more land/energy than farming crops/ Provides a lower yield than farming crops; false; because some traditional grazing land is not suitable for growing crops (e.g. rocky hillsides)/some livestock can graze in conservation areas on the brink of desertification which is unable to be cultivated.

For answers to the Practice Papers, visit: www.scholastic.co.uk/gcse